FIND
LOVE

FIND LOVE

HOW TO NAVIGATE MODERN LOVE AND DISCOVER THE RIGHT PARTNER FOR YOU

PAUL C. BRUNSON

Vermilion/Happy Place, an imprint of Ebury Publishing
20 Vauxhall Bridge Road
London SW1V 2SA

Vermilion is part of the Penguin Random House group of companies
whose addresses can be found at global.penguinrandomhouse.com

Copyright © Paul C. Brunson 2024
Cowriter: Paul Murphy

Paul C. Brunson has asserted his right to be identified
as the author of this Work in accordance with the
Copyright, Designs and Patents Act 1988

First published by Vermilion in 2024

www.penguin.co.uk

A CIP catalogue record for this book is
available from the British Library

ISBN 9781785044687

Typeset in 11/17.9pt Swift LT Pro by Jouve (UK), Milton Keynes
Printed and bound in Great Britain by Clays Ltd, Elcograf S.p.A.

The authorised representative in the EEA is Penguin Random House
Ireland, Morrison Chambers, 32 Nassau Street, Dublin D02 YH68

*For the keepers of my spirit, the fuel of my passion
and the extension of my thoughts*

Modern dating can feel like a minefield . . . but it doesn't have to be. In *Find Love*, world-renowned relationship expert Paul Brunson provides you with vital advice for navigating and securing real and lasting connections.

Whether you're single and looking for love or in a relationship and wondering if your partner is 'the one', this book will arm you with the advice, skills and simple tools you need to make an informed decision on how to simultaneously love yourself and find the right partner for you.

CONTENTS

Introduction   1

Chapter 1 From Arranged Marriages to
           Attachment Theory and Beyond   11
Chapter 2 The Power of Our Pasts and
           the Hidden Factors that Shape
           Our Relationships   39
Chapter 3 A Strong Sense of Self Is the Key
           to a Successful Relationship   67
Chapter 4 How Your Environment Shapes Your
           Search for a Partner   89
Chapter 5 The Pros and Cons of
           Different Ways to Meet a Partner   115
Chapter 6 Maximising Your Chances of
           Finding a Partner   147
Chapter 7 Green Flags: The Five Fundamentals
           You Should Be Looking for in a
           Partner   171

Chapter 8 Red Flags: How to Identify Toxic
           Partners   197
Chapter 9 Are You Ready for Forever?
           Understanding the Signs of
           Commitment Readiness   223

           The Long-Term Relationship
           Satisfaction Scale (LRSS)   245
           Resources   261
           Notes   265
           About the Author   275

INTRODUCTION

Looking for love can be one of the most exciting and rewarding experiences in life, but it can also be a difficult and frustrating journey. It's not always easy to tell if someone is a good match for you, and it's normal to feel overwhelmed or unsure where to begin. But don't worry — I've spent most of my adult life studying relationships. Understanding the data behind love is the only thing I enjoy more than love itself. I've worked as one of the world's most well-known matchmakers and couples' counsellors for over a decade, I give relationship talks around the world, I co-hosted one of the world's largest social experiments on love with Oprah Winfrey, I am an expert on the popular dating shows *Celebs Go Dating* and *Married at First Sight UK*, and I'm proud to be Tinder's Global Relationship Insights Expert, which gives me access to more data on how we choose partners than any study in the world. I'm therefore expertly placed to help you find love.

The first of a three-book series about the fundamentals of love, *Find Love* focuses on one of life's most important decisions: choosing a partner. Selecting the right person is the foundation of a successful and happy relationship, so it's critical that you get it right. Whether you're single and looking for love or in a relationship and wondering if your partner is 'the one', this book will arm you with the information, skills and tools you need to make an informed decision.

One of the main reasons I wanted to write this book was because I think there's a void in the space around relationship advice. Historically, there's been a lot of what I feel is knee-jerk advice from the people we know — a friend, colleague or auntie, say — who have had some life experience, not always positive. And their advice is based solely on their own interactions and the three or four relationships they have had — and that's it. That's where a lot of relationship advice has traditionally come from. Then, within the last twenty years or so, relationship sciences have come to the fore, with evolutionary psychology in particular beginning to examine romantic relationships from a scientific point of view, albeit with a focus mainly on straight partner-ships thus far.*

So, we've had the aunties on one side, and now we have the sciences on the other. And the challenge is that the scientists are writing for each other — it sometimes feels like you need a PhD to interpret what they're saying. Whereas the advice coming from the other side doesn't have the same depth of research or as much sup-porting evidence to back it up.

I have a unique perspective to be able to bridge that gap. To take you back to the beginning, my parents were in a loving relationship. When I was a young boy, we moved from New York to Virginia. Our old neighbourhood was full of nuclear families. When we got to Virginia, almost none of the kids in our housing development lived with both parents — they typically just lived with their mums. And people would poke fun at me because I lived with my mother and father. At first, I wondered if my set-up was strange. I soon realised, however, how lucky I was, and that by observing my parents and seeing how they managed their emotions and relationship, I

---

* More work is starting to be done on same-sex relationships, but this has yet to catch up with the breadth of research available on partner-ships between straight men and women.

was learning skills. In high school, I became the go-to person who everybody would ask questions about sex and relationships.

Then, when I went to college, I very quickly entered into a committed relationship with the woman who would become my wife. And people would always come to me and Jill for advice. It was just a bit of fun, but I also found myself gravitating towards psychology and learning more about how relationships work. After college, my first job was as a researcher in an investment bank. Although the focus was finance, I was a researcher first and foremost.

In 2008, Jill and I decided to take our interest in relationships and launch a matchmaking business. Before this, we had been living between Washington, DC and Istanbul, and I was working for a Turkish billionaire named Enver Yücel, managing his investments in the USA. I also had a non-profit organisation that I ran on the weekends to help underserved kids from New York to Atlanta. One of our programmes was a summer camp, where we'd invite 100 mostly Black and Latino high-school kids to attend and work on their maths, science and English. In the summer of 2008, I was at the camp helping to check in the students, and one of the questions we asked them was how many parents lived in their households. Out of the 100 students, not one said they lived with both their parents, and there was almost no male representation in any of their homes. It was mind-blowing to me — I couldn't believe it.

This was when I recognised a deeper problem than just helping these kids with their studies. It was apparent to me that we were focusing on the challenges in these kids' lives at school, but having a parent missing was potentially an even larger challenge for them, and that was when I began to think about the power of strong relationships, which was the seed idea behind the matchmaking business. By the end of that summer, Jill and I were inviting our single friends round to play a relationship game that we had created. Before long, one of the couples had gotten engaged. So I put my business hat on and said, 'Oh, this is interesting. We should license this game to someone.'

After doing a bit of research, we discovered that there was such a thing as professional matchmaking. I then tried to track down a well-known matchmaker in an attempt to sell her our house-party game, but she never responded to me. I saw somewhere that she would be at a matchmaking conference in New York, so I booked a ticket to attend, planning to sell her or someone else our game. I got there late and sat in the back of a session with 250 of the world's top matchmakers and saw something that would change my life. I was one of the youngest. I was the only man. I was the only Black person. And I thought, 'Wow, instead of selling this idea, I have a unique voice that I could bring to this industry.' And I quit my job in Istanbul, and that's how Jill and I got into the matchmaking space.

That led to us working with clients rather than just setting up our friends. Through that work, we came to understand the emotion that's attached to the decisions people make when choosing a partner, and why it's so challenging. But we were missing the research part. That's when we started to apply what we were learning from relationship science to our matchmaking. I am now at the point where I believe I have an even more unique POV in the relationship space, because I'm a trained researcher, I spent ten years as a professional matchmaker and counsellor, I have worked as both a mentor and instructor to therapists, dating coaches and matchmakers around the world, I appear as the resident relationship expert on the top morning shows in the UK and USA, and I provide global relationship insights for the biggest dating app in the world. In addition, I'm happily married — my wife is my best friend — and I'm a parent. All of these pieces add up to give me an original perspective. I'm not saying it's better, but it is different, and it is why I am in a strong position to bring together the anecdotal and the scientific to help you on your relationship journey.

♥

In the pages that follow, you'll learn where to look for love, how to recognise the five fundamentals that make someone a good partner who will help you to be your best self, how to spot red flags so that you can avoid people you should never get involved with, and how to navigate the world of love with confidence. You'll also learn how to overcome common dating stumbling blocks and how to build a solid foundation with your partner.

But that isn't all. This book also includes real-life examples to help you put the advice into action. You'll learn how to assess your own needs and desires, how to address and overcome any romantic trauma in your life and how to judge whether someone is ready to be in a long-term relationship with you. Beyond this, I am incredibly excited to include a completely new and bespoke tool that will help you to use the knowledge you will gain from reading this book and put it into practice — the Long-Term Relationship Satisfaction Scale (LRSS), which I have developed with Dr Angela Smith and Hannah Mohsen and tested on more than 800 respondents.

Angela is a forensic and behavioural psychologist, and an expert in the field of resilience and psychological matching. She has been featured on numerous popular television shows and helps people find their perfect match using her unique combination of skills and insights. Her expertise has helped many couples create long-lasting relationships. Hannah is a psychologist with more than ten years of experience and is the managing director of Open Door Performance, a coaching, training and well-being consultancy. Her speciality lies in psychometric testing and behavioural interventions. She is also a regular behind-the-scenes expert on TV dating shows, where she uses her psychology background to support contributors. We have brought our skills and breadth of experience together to come up with an assessment scale which will empower you to approach your search for love with rationality and help you to take control of a process that so many of us find challenging but which couldn't be more important – who you choose to commit to in the long term.

Throughout my career, I've witnessed at first hand the difficulties people face in their pursuit of love. I've also seen the effectiveness of the right strategies and techniques in assisting people in finding and maintaining happy, healthy relationships. And I'm not just talking about my clients; I've used these strategies in my own marriage, which after more than twenty years is stronger than ever.

This book is for anyone looking for true love and a long-lasting, committed, fulfilling relationship, regardless of sexual orientation. That could be a marriage, but it could equally be a couple who simply want to live with one another and build their lives together. Or it could be someone who wants a polyamorous but committed relationship with multiple partners. There are no boundaries on what that relationship might look like.

Whatever you are looking for, the insights and advice in this book will help you to find the partner and happiness you deserve. So don't put it off any longer. Begin your journey today and let me guide you on the path to finding true love.

'OUR NEEDS MIGHT HAVE CHANGED OVER TIME, BUT CHOOSING THE RIGHT PARTNER HAS ALWAYS BEEN DIFFICULT AND THE CONSEQUENCES HAVE ALWAYS BEEN IMPORTANT'

1

FROM ARRANGED MARRIAGES TO ATTACHMENT THEORY AND BEYOND

The aim of this book is to help you find love today, but to do this it is first helpful to understand how relationships have changed over the years. The reason I think it's important to look at the history of relationships is because it helps provide context to the modern dating scene. If you asked them, most people would probably say that it's never been harder to find a partner than it is now. Whereas if you were to talk to my grandmother who grew up in a very small town in Jamaica, in what she would call 'a bush within the bush', she would say it was never harder to find someone than when she was young. The truth is, it's not necessarily harder today — the challenges are just different.

I believe that a big part of the reason why we have always found it difficult to find a suitable partner is because relationships are such an important aspect of what makes us human. There is, therefore, a lot riding on finding someone who fulfils our needs. But what do I mean by 'needs' in this context?

Developmental psychologist Abraham Maslow proposed his theory of the hierarchy of needs in the 1940s. This concept is most often expressed as a diagram of a pyramid, with the most basic human needs at the bottom and the increasingly complex ones further up. The definition of these needs has been refined and debated over the years, but at its most basic, there are five levels, with physiological needs (like food and shelter) at the base of the pyramid, followed by safety (such as good health and protection from danger), love and belongingness (including intimate relationships and friendships), self-esteem (for instance, respect and recognition) and self-actualisation (sometimes referred to as 'reaching your full potential').[1]

The history of partnership reaches from today all the way back to hunter-gatherer days and can be viewed with this hierarchy in mind.[2] In prehistoric days, the priority when it came to relationships was most likely fulfilling the lower-level physiological and safety needs.

Fast-forward to today, and it's no longer just about finding someone to help you survive and remain safe, although safety is still an inherent part of relationships. Now, we're looking to achieve the higher-level needs: how can my partner help me to become self-actualised?

So, when people today say that it's never been harder to find a partner, I tell them to pause for a moment. In the hunter-gatherer days, who you chose as a partner would contribute to whether or not you would survive another day, week or month. Was there a lot of weight on that decision? Hell, yeah. That's a life-or-death decision. Our needs might have changed over time, but choosing the right partner has always been difficult and the consequences have always been important.

Today, we have different challenges, one of the biggest of which, in my opinion, is the paradox of choice.[3] We believe that we have endless options when we're choosing a partner. A dating app like Tinder, which is the largest in the world, has been downloaded more than 530 million times, and it is easy to feel paralysed by the thought that you have to sift through that massive pool of people to find the right one for you. My grandmother in Jamaica had maybe eight men in her village to choose from. If she jumped on a dating app now, she would probably find it completely overwhelming.

The idea that you have endless choice does several things. One result is that each choice has less value, as you can just select again if you make a bad decision. And it can also become even harder to make a choice in the first place. And that's detrimental when it comes to relationships. But choice is good — a wide selection of options puts you in control and encourages you to step outside of your dating comfort zone — hence the paradox.

Another big change that has happened over time is the expectation we place on our partners.[4] In his book *The All-or-Nothing Marriage*, psychologist Eli Finkel says there have been three phases of marriage over the last 400 years or so.* The first type was the institutional or pragmatic marriage, characterised, for example, by economic stability and protection from violence. The next stage was marriage for companionship and love, which came with the rise of the middle classes in the post-industrial age in the mid-nineteenth century. This phase saw the emergence of the idea of the soulmate and romance. And finally, from about 1965 onwards, we moved into a stage of the self-expressive marriage. People now expect their

---

* He's writing specifically about marriages in the USA, but I think his ideas are applicable to committed relationships across all of the so-called WEIRD (Western, Educated, Industrialised, Rich and Democratic) nations.

relationships to be fulfilling in every way: practically, emotionally and sexually.[5]

In other words, we now place more expectation on and want more from our partners. And because we place more expectation on them, the stakes feel higher and there's more pressure to find the right match. In the past, people did not expect to find fulfilment in one person. It took a village to fulfil your needs. Perhaps one person in your life satisfied your intellectual needs, another your sexual needs and someone else your sense of companionship. The point is, you went to the person you were married to for perhaps one or two of the myriad needs you had, whereas today the idea is to find one person to fulfil all your needs simultaneously.

If you choose to find a partner to satisfy all your needs, it's important to recognise that it will be more challenging to identify that partner than one who can satisfy just some. On the flipside, if you decide to pursue a partner who only satisfies some of your needs, you can't question why they're not delivering further down the line.

Another thing that's changed drastically over time is the empowerment of women. This really began to take off in the 1960s with the introduction of things like the contraceptive pill and time-saving household appliances, such as the washing machine. These innovations helped to liberate women from the domestic sphere, and from that point onwards we've seen improved education, income and choice for women, to the point where women now initiate divorce more often than men (69 per cent of the time).[6] And going hand-in-hand with this has been society's increased acceptance of a wider variety of relationships, whether that be same-sex, polyamorous, interracial or interreligious.

The involvement of the state in our love lives has also changed over the years, with governments really getting behind the institution of marriage in particular. This increased role of the state has come at the expense of the church, which has basically disappeared completely in terms of being a conduit for marriage, when at one point it was the number-one factor in the forging and sustaining of partnerships.

I would even go as far as to say that we are entering a new phase beyond Finkel's idea of the self-expressive marriage, which I like to call the 'relationship information deluge'. There's more content and we're more informed about relationships than ever before. In my opinion, the top three types of content that people consume are about politics, sports and relationships. You just have to look at the popularity of television shows like *Married at First Sight*. I've been on TV for about twelve years now, and back when I started, not even the experts referred to psychological terms on these types of shows. Compare that with today and the cast members themselves are talking about gaslighting, toxicity and attachment styles. There's now a whole other level of information about relationships.

As a result of being better informed about relationships, it drastically shifts how you choose to pick a partner — you become choosier. And not only do you become choosier, but you might convince yourself that you're not interested in pursuing a relationship that could actually have merit. The bottom line is that being informed increases our level of expectation, and that then results in us either not choosing a relationship or in us hitting the eject button, sometimes prematurely.

When researchers look at satisfaction rates, people overall are less happy in their relationships than they were thirty years ago. And it's precisely because we weren't so aware of what was possible and our expectations from what a partner could give us were lower. The roles our partners played were limited, and we only went to them for a few of our diverse needs. However, the top 20 per cent of most-satisfied marriages are now more satisfied than thirty years ago. And why is that? Because they are more aware of what they want, and they're using all of their tools to get it.[7]

And that's the purpose of this book — to equip you with the knowledge and tools to better understand the relationship landscape so you can go out and identify the strongest partner for you. I firmly believe the number-one reason for relationships failing is because we pick bad partners. If you pick the right partner, if you have expectations and share the same goals, you can have higher levels of relationship satisfaction, but you can also be more satisfied generally. That's what leads to living longer. That's what leads to higher income. That's what leads to being healthier. That's what leads to you getting more enjoyment out of life.[8]

ATTACHMENT THEORY

Making bad decisions and being unsatisfied with your relationship is going to have an impact on every aspect of your life. As I said, being in a strong relationship is such a core aspect of being human. If you look at the loneliness epidemic, the increased cost of living, the COVID pandemic, all have contributed to the challenges around people's mental health today. However, one of the number-one drivers of our well-being, and one which is arguably not recognised so readily, is our relationships. And not just our relationships today, but our relationships from the past and what they've taught us.

This is the reason why attachment theory is so popular now. An area of psychological investigation since the 1960s, it originally focused on the impact of the relationships between young children and their primary caregivers. Then, from the 1980s onwards, researchers such as Sue Johnson, and Cindy Hazan and Phillip Shaver, developed the concept further and applied it to adult relationships. They found that there are many similarities between attachment theory in children and adults, and many psychologists argue that attachments formed in our early years influence our attachment styles as we grow up.[9]

There are four categories of attachment in adults: secure, anxious — preoccupied, dismissive — avoidant and fearful — avoidant.[10] These closely follow the three childhood categories of secure, anxious — ambivalent and avoidant, with the exception that the avoidant category is further differentiated and split in two in adults.

SECURE

Those with a secure attachment style generally have a positive view of themselves and other people. As a result, they find it relatively easy to form close emotional connections, and they are happy to depend on others and have others depend on them. They also tend to have high self-esteem and not worry too much about what other people think of them.

Those with a secure attachment style have been found to have higher relationship satisfaction in general. Although the reasons for this need further research, one theory is that they are better communicators and more open to revealing their true selves. In addition, people with secure attachment styles are thought to have better strategies for managing conflict, find it easier to express their emotions, and have a higher perception of support from their partners, all of which lead to stronger relationships. And because they tend to be more committed, those relationships are longer-lasting on average too.

People with the three insecure attachment styles, on the other hand, find close relationships more challenging, and they are more susceptible to things like depression and anxiety.

ANXIOUS–PREOCCUPIED

Those who are anxious — preoccupied tend to think poorly of themselves and highly of others. They seek emotional intimacy but doubt that other people will want or be able to love them, and they can be needy and uncomfortable without the safety blanket of a close relationship. They also worry that they value other people more than other people value them. This can lead to them becoming overly dependent on others and exhibiting high levels of emotionality, anxiety and impulsiveness, which perhaps explains why anxious — preoccupied people can sometimes stay in unhappy relationships for a long time.

DISMISSIVE–AVOIDANT

In terms of the two avoidant attachment styles in adults, those who are dismissive generally have a positive view of themselves and a low opinion of others. They shy away from close relationships, placing higher value on independence and self-sufficiency. This can result in them being defensive and hiding their true feelings. They also tend to distance themselves from their attachments if they suspect they are going to be rejected.

FEARFUL–AVOIDANT

Those who are fearful — avoidant, meanwhile, don't usually have a set sense of themselves or others, and they are not comfortable forming close relationships, even though they want them. This is partly because they find it difficult to trust people and are fearful of being hurt, leading to them feeling unworthy, suppressing their emotions and finding it difficult to be affectionate.[11]

In their brilliant book *Attached*, Dr Amir Levine and psychologist Rachel Heller investigate attachment theory in detail, describing how we are shaped by the love we received from the people we value most, which in turn influences our current relationships.[12] And it's not just what our parents did when we were two — every relationship we have has an impact. If you're in a relationship with someone who is a severe avoidant and you are secure, given enough time you will shift out of your secure attachment. So every relationship you've had impacts not just how you show up in the world, but also how you react to adversity, which is why emotional resilience is so important in terms of deciding on a partner (see Chapter 7).

And although this applies to all of our relationships, our romantic relationships are the most important. This is why who you choose to go out on a date with or who you choose to have sex with or who you choose to hang out with can have a real impact. The reality is that decision can change the course of your life.

To give you an idea of what attachment style might best describe your approach to relationships, you can use the following table.

Attachment style	Self-reflection questions
Secure	♥ Do you feel comfortable with intimacy and closeness? ♥ Are you typically warm and loving in your relationships? ♥ Do you find it easy to trust others and don't often worry about being abandoned or about someone getting too close to you? ♥ Are you comfortable depending on others and having others depend on you?
Anxious—preoccupied	♥ Do you often feel that your desire for closeness and intimacy is not reciprocated at the same level by your partner? ♥ Do you often worry that your partner doesn't really love you or won't want to stay with you? ♥ Do you feel a strong need for validation and reassurance from others? ♥ Are you anxious and insecure about your relationships?

Attachment style	Self-reflection questions
Dismissive—avoidant	♥ Do you feel a need to maintain emotional distance in your relationships? ♥ Do you feel uncomfortable when people get too close and often create distance? ♥ Do you pride yourself on being self-reliant and independent to the point of avoiding close relationships? ♥ Do you often suppress and hide your feelings?
Fearful—avoidant	♥ Do you have mixed feelings about close relationships, both desiring closeness and feeling uncomfortable with it? ♥ Do you find it difficult to trust people or depend on them, fearing that you will be hurt? ♥ Do you often feel that you will be rejected, yet struggle to cut ties with others? ♥ Are you fearful of getting too emotionally attached because the person might leave?

THE COMPONENTS OF LOVE

To my mind, romantic love has three components. The first is friendship — you need to be with someone you can confide in and who can confide in you. You like their company and want to spend time with them, and they want to spend time with you. The next piece is intimacy. This could include physical intimacy, although it doesn't have to. Instead, I'm talking primarily about emotional intimacy — someone you can be completely vulnerable with. We all have a public life, a private life and a secret life. The intimate partner knows your secret life. It's the person you feel emotionally safe with and can therefore be physically intimate with if you so choose. And last but not least, you have commitment, which is simply knowing that the person who stands arm-in-arm with you today is the same person who's going to stand arm-in-arm with you tomorrow. So, if you have friendship, intimacy and commitment, you have romantic love.

For some people, a long-term partnership today can still be transactional. It could simply mean that I'm signing up to provide you with financial security, and you're signing up to take care of the home. We're going to engage in this relationship, but we don't have to be emotionally intimate, and we don't have to be friendly. My aim, however, is to help you find a long-term partnership that is based on the conception of romantic love I just outlined. And by doing so, you can become your best self.

It's like Michelangelo's work process. He wouldn't look at a piece of stone and say, 'All right, I'm going to carve this beautiful piece of art.' He'd look at the stone and say, 'I'm going to release the art that's already within it.' That's what a great relationship is. You have a partner who helps to release your optimal self, whatever that might be.

That doesn't mean you should wait to fall in love to find your true self. The best time to work on your relationship or marriage is before it begins, and this involves getting to a good place in the other aspects of your life (see Chapter 3). Then, it's about defining what a loving relationship means to you and what it is that you're looking for. Many people, particularly straight women, wait to be chosen. Once selected, they look to their partner and say, 'Well, what do you want?' And their partner says, 'Well, what do *you* want?' And then they live out what they've decided and realise it's not what either of them wanted. It's much better to say ahead of time, 'OK, based on who I know I am, what do I need in a relationship to thrive?' Then, when you start engaging with potential partners in the dating process, you've already outlined what your boundaries are.

A lot of people don't like to draw parallels between a job interview and finding love, but there are so many similarities. If you are advertising a job as the employer, you don't just say, 'Hey, does anybody want to come to work for me?' Instead, you outline the role and responsibilities and describe the characteristics you are looking for in the successful candidate. This is only possible because you have done the work prior to the interview process, and you understand what is required. Defining what love is, what it means to you and what you are looking for is the work you have to do before embarking on a relationship, as it empowers you to make better choices.

The next thing to realise is that there's short-term mating, and there's long-term mating. One of the biggest problems in the dating landscape is that people don't define it that way — you just have people dating or seeing one another. The second problem is that you have people who want short-term going after the people who want long-term relationships and people who want long-term going after people who are only looking for short-term interactions. Often this is because people haven't come up with the language to categorise themselves and haven't worked out what they're actually looking for.

On Tinder, one of the first things you do is identify your relationship goal. There are six options: do you want a long-term relationship? Do you want a short-term relationship? Do you want a short-term relationship but you're open to a long-term relationship? Do you want a long-term relationship but are open to a short-term relationship? Are you just looking for a friend? And are you not sure what you're looking for? By far the number-one selected option is 'long-term partner'. Number two is 'long-term, but open to short', which has become very popular in recent years. This is sometimes called 'probation', especially on platforms like TikTok, the idea being that I'll give you three months and if things are working, we'll consider long-term. There's a challenge in this because the strategies that you would use to find a long-term partner don't necessarily translate to short-term. And this can lead to confusion. Short-term can mean casual sex, or maybe it's just hanging out and there's no intimacy, not even emotional intimacy.

The younger you are, the more likely it is that you'll be interested in short-term. If you've just come out of a long-term relationship, you might also be more likely to want short-term. So even within short-term, there's a variety of relationship forms, and not knowing what you want or pursuing someone who has very different relationship goals can lead to conflict and hurt. The point of confusion comes from not really knowing what you want. You're trying to cover all bases by saying you want short-to-long-term, but because this could mean so many different things, it's not as likely that the other person is going to have the same goals as you in that situation.

Another challenge is the fear of missing out. If you act like you want a long-term partnership, you might worry that you're going to scare people off. A lot of women fall into this category. They think that guys are just looking for sex, so they say they want short-term because the man does, and then hope that they'll get him to stay.

The drive behind this approach is once again not doing the work, and not feeling confident enough in the decisions you're making. And one of the main reasons why I think people are not confident making decisions for themselves is because they don't have a vision for what it is they want or don't have belief that they will be able to reach their end goal. And so they therefore make a poor decision on the front end and say they are open to short-term when they really aren't. My aim is to help you to make good decisions right from the outset.

IT TAKES A VILLAGE

As a matchmaker, I find arranged marriages fascinating. I have a buddy from Pakistan, and whenever I hang out with him, I always ask him about them. Two of the most interesting things he's told me are: the separation rate in arranged marriages is on average less than the divorce rate overall; and the satisfaction rate among women in arranged marriages is higher than it is on average in non-arranged marriages. Both of these facts are backed up by academic studies.[13] But why is this the case? Yes, there is a cultural aspect at play here, but a big part of it comes down to support networks and having people around you who can help you and make you feel confident enough to express all the things you need to express — it takes a village, right? Because when we are deciding on a partner, one thing that we often don't want to acknowledge is that we can be irrational when it comes to love. One of the ways to mitigate this is to consult people whom you trust and who can be more objective to help you make the decision.[14]

When my wife and I had our matchmaking agency, we pioneered the 360-degree interview in the dating industry. When a client came to us, before we would ask them any questions, we would request contact information for a friend, family member, employee, boss or co-worker, and previous romantic interests. The idea was to get a 360-degree perspective of the client and a true understanding of who that person was from people who knew them well. Because of cognitive dissonance (when your actions and behaviour don't align with your values or beliefs), we don't fully understand who we are. And we don't understand what we need. But it turns out that your friends and family, the people in your support network, have a really good idea of who you are and what you need.

Your support network is not only there to help you make the initial decision about who is right for you — they are also there to support the relationship in the future and help you make the decisions that inevitably come up over time. Of course, it can get to a point where it becomes cumbersome to consult other people all the time, and you absolutely need to be able to make your own decisions. But having a support network is really important.

One of the reasons why *Married at First Sight* has become such a successful franchise, and why there's so much interest in it, is because there's a group aspect to it. When I started on the show in 2019, the couples would get married and the cameras would track them as they lived their lives separately from the other couples. Then the format changed. The couples would get married and go on honeymoon but would then move into an apartment building with the other newlyweds. And every week they would meet for a dinner party and for a commitment ceremony in front of the experts. That's what increased the show's popularity. Every series, the audience wants more dinner parties and more commitment ceremonies.

The reason for this is in part to do with the law of proximity. A couple living on their own is more likely to get along, because the more you have novel experiences with someone, the higher the likelihood that you're going to bond with them. The moment you introduce other couples into the equation, they start to compare their relationships and can even become competitive. Or perhaps they are attracted to someone else on the show. As soon as you create a group experience, it becomes unpredictable.

The couples that typically end up making it are the couples that gain the support of the village. As I'm writing this book, I'm also filming a series of *Married at First*

Sight UK, and we're actually going through that right now. A couple pissed off the whole group and realised that their relationship was suffering as a result. They then spent the next two weeks trying to work themselves back into the good graces of the group. We are social animals. We cannot survive and thrive without the support of a network.[15]

It's tough to be alone. When my wife and I moved from the USA to the UK, we left our friends and family behind. Losing this support network meant that we lost value and had to take more on our shoulders. As a couple, as caregivers, we had to balance more. If we had an emergency, or even if we just wanted to be able to go on a date, we couldn't fall back on our family and friends any more; we only had ourselves to rely on.

Over the years, research has also shown that the number of people we consider to be our close friends, the sort of people who you could call at 3am and ask for help, has decreased, particularly with men. People have gone from having on average five close friends to having only two or three, and many men have no one who would fall into that category. This is a big problem. And it's an even bigger issue when it comes to our relationships, because it means that a man likely has no one to advise him. He has no one to help him make what I consider to be the most important decision of his life: who to choose as a partner. Thought leaders from various industries, such as Warren Buffett, Sheryl Sandberg and Esther Perel, have all echoed this and said that the most important decision in the world is who you choose as a partner, and most people are now making that decision on their own without rational input.

Thirty, forty and fifty years ago, it was not a solo decision at all. It was probably the main topic of conversation among your friends and family for weeks and weeks. And then they would be there to help you with the other big decisions too: where are you going to live? Should you have a child? When should you have that child? What school should they go to? And all of these decisions ended up shaping not just our lives but our children's lives. Without the same level of support as we had in the past, it inevitably leads to poor decisions.

The solution to this is something I've mentioned already, and which we'll return to several times over the course of this book — the best time to work on your relationship is before it begins. Strengthen your support network before you get involved with someone romantically. If you don't have a support network, can you build one? It's not necessarily easy if you're more of an introverted person, but there are lots of avenues to help you connect with people. If you are someone who has no 3am friends and is on a dating app on average six or seven hours a day, spending five of those building your support network instead would probably benefit you more in the long term, in your future relationship and in life more generally.

People ask me all the time, 'Where do I find a partner?' And I always say, 'Go to your friends and family, or, even better, people in your extended network, and tell them that you want them to set you up on three blind dates.' And do you know what? Almost everyone pushes back and says they don't feel comfortable asking for this kind of help. They're not activating their networks. Because not only do you have to identify and nurture your networks, you have to activate them too.* And to sustain friendship, you have to exert energy, but this is a lifelong investment with massive returns.[16]

Understanding how relationships have changed over the years might not seem all that important at first, but I would argue that the better informed you are, the better decisions you can make. By looking to the past, we equip

---

* I'll go into more detail about ways to do this when I discuss how important it is to strengthen weak ties later in the book.

ourselves to navigate today's dating landscape, as there is no point trying to find love as though we are still living in the 1950s, before the seismic societal and technological changes that have happened since then. And you're limiting your chances of success if your only source of advice and support comes from non-expert friends and family. Instead, I want to help you maximise your ability to find the perfect partner, which starts with knowing how we got to where we are today and then utilising all of the resources at your disposal. We can then move on to the next step in the process, which also involves looking to the past, but this time a bit closer to home.

KEY TAKEAWAYS

1. As relationships have changed over time, people have increasingly wanted more from their partners.

2. Understanding your attachment style, as influenced by your past relationships, can help you to choose your partner wisely.

3. There is a big difference between short-term and long-term mating, so it is vital that you identify and clearly communicate what your relationship goal is.

'BEFORE THINKING ABOUT TRYING TO FIND AN IDEAL PARTNER, IT IS BENEFICIAL TO IDENTIFY THE TRAUMA YOU'VE EXPERIENCED, RECOGNISE YOUR ATTACHMENT STYLE AND BEGIN TO SELF-HEAL'

2

THE POWER OF OUR PASTS AND THE HIDDEN FACTORS THAT SHAPE OUR RELATIONSHIPS

Understanding how relationships have changed over time is just one part of the process. Taking a retrospective look at your own relationship history is also a really important tool in understanding what's gone wrong in the past, what's gone right and what it is that you're looking for in the future. At the same time, it's also vital to identify the other external forces that influence us as we try to navigate the dating landscape.

In the last chapter, I spoke a bit about the rise of attachment theory over the past twenty years or so, and it is unarguably a valuable lens through which we can view relationships. However, attachment theory has now become so popular that I suspect we are ready to move a step beyond it and talk about how attachment and trauma are intertwined. By trauma, I mean a significant event that causes us distress, and that distress then sits with us and causes psychological and physiological change. Dr Gabor Maté, a physician who specialises in trauma, argues that trauma and the stress caused by it is, for example, a key component of addiction.[1] How we recognise and manage trauma therefore has an unprecedented impact on us and our relationships, as does the trauma we neglect. Many of us like to point the finger outwards to what our partner or potential partners have problems dealing with, when in reality one of the biggest issues is the fact that we haven't acknowledged and dealt with our own trauma.

TYPES OF TRAUMA

INTERGENERATIONAL TRAUMA

There are various types of trauma that are relevant here, the first being intergenerational. It's perhaps not talked about as much as some of the other types, potentially because it's not so easily observed. But here in the UK, I can see the Second World War, for example, has had a substantial impact on the children of that generation, but also on the grandchildren who are still dealing with the trauma that was not addressed, due to the stiff-upper-lip, sweep-it-under-the-rug mentality typically associated with the Brits. Other examples would be the transatlantic slave trade and the Holocaust. All of these historic events and systemic issues have pushed trauma through to us today that we might not even be aware of.

EARLY-LIFE TRAUMA

The second type of trauma is that caused by the relationships we have with our first caregivers, whether that be our parents, grandparents or guardians. The trauma-causing behaviours that are most damaging are those that are intentional, such as physical abuse, which can result in severe injuries as well as emotional distress and long-lasting psychological effects; emotional or psychological abuse, including constant criticism, humiliation and manipulation, which can lead to low self-esteem, anxiety and depression; verbal abuse, which can cause emotional trauma and erode self-worth; and sexual abuse, which can cause deep emotional scars, confusion and long-term trauma. But unintentional behaviours can also have serious consequences. For example, neglect, when caregivers fail to provide adequate care, attention or emotional support to their children, can lead to feelings of abandonment and insecurity, and inconsistent or unpredictable parenting can create confusion and a sense of instability. A lack of boundary-setting can result in people struggling to understand limits and manage their behaviour, and overprotection, or helicopter parenting, while well intentioned, can hinder independence, self-confidence and an ability to handle challenges. It is these early traumas, whether intentional or not, that impact how we attach to other people and initially inform whether we are anxious, avoidant or secure (see page 18).

TRAUMA FROM FRIENDSHIPS AND CASUAL RELATIONSHIPS

The next type of trauma arises from all the relationships we have, platonic as well as romantic. As adults, we don't spend enough time thinking about, or don't give enough value or credit to, the impact that these important interactions have on us. In terms of the platonic relationships we have, the friends, family and colleagues that make up our village have a huge impact on our lives. This can be positive, like when they support us when it comes to making good choices about who to choose as a partner, but they can also impart trauma and distress — an example of this might be bullying or discrimination in the workplace. And then there is the impact of our casual romantic relationships. I often hear people say things like, 'Oh, it doesn't matter if I just have sex with her,' or, 'I just want to have fun with him, and it doesn't matter that he's toxic and a narcissist.' Well, actually it does — it can create trauma that you carry with you into your future relationships.

TRAUMA FROM LONG-TERM ROMANTIC RELATIONSHIPS

The fourth type of trauma is that which occurs in our committed romantic relationships, which can of course be substantial — many of us have had our hearts broken at some point in our lives. This type of trauma can show up in different ways depending on your circumstances and experiences. Emotional or psychological trauma can occur when an individual has been subjected to persistent emotional abuse, manipulation or neglect. Examples could include constant belittling, shaming, gaslighting or stonewalling. This can lead to low self-esteem, feelings of worthlessness, and difficulties with trust and intimacy in future relationships. Physical trauma involves any form of physical abuse, such as hitting, slapping, punching or any other action that inflicts physical harm, and can leave the victim in a constant state of fear and anxiety, particularly when it comes to romantic attachments in the future. Sexual trauma occurs when an individual has been forced into non-consensual sexual activities. This can lead to difficulties with intimacy, trust and sexual dysfunction. It can also cause feelings of shame and guilt. Relational trauma occurs when trust is violated within a relationship, such as through infidelity or betrayal. This can lead to difficulties trusting people, as well as feelings of jealousy and insecurity in future relationships. Finally, complex trauma happens when someone experiences multiple traumatic events over a long period, often within the context of a relationship. This might include a combination of emotional, physical or sexual trauma, or other forms of abuse. The effect of complex trauma is cumulative, and it can have a profound and long-lasting impact on an individual's mental health and ability to form healthy relationships.

I once worked with someone who had, one way or another, suffered from all four types of trauma in his past. To begin with, his grandfather never talked about what had happened to him when he returned from the Second World War. Instead, he turned to drugs and alcohol as his coping mechanisms, and he abused his wife and family. This behaviour was then passed down to his son. The grandson was observant of all of this behaviour and, as a consequence, believed that you showed love by holding in emotion. That sharing was weakness and keeping things to yourself was strength. That you loved by sometimes acting out physically to your partner, because it demonstrated that you were passionate. And you self-soothed with alcohol and drugs instead of self-compassion.

He also had an anxious attachment style because he was loved one second and hit the next. And it wasn't just the relationship he had with his father that helped to form this attachment style. His aunts and uncles suffered the same generational trauma, and they operated in the same way. This led to him becoming super anxious and hypervigilant. Then, by the time he was ready to have relationships, whether platonic or romantic, who was he attracted to? The risk-takers and hedonists, people who typically shied away from deeper, more emotional connections. He got into a lot of trouble when he was younger and engaged in very risky sexual behaviours when he was only sixteen or seventeen years old. He never admitted to physical abuse, but he became an emotional abuser, a characteristic that often occurs in people who are anxious.

When he came to see me, he said, 'You know what? None of these women really love me. They all just want to use me.' As a result of not understanding how the trauma he'd experienced had shaped him, he was completely confused as to the role he'd played in his relationships. In essence, not acknowledging or dealing with his trauma meant he wasn't ready to be in a relationship without bringing toxicity to it.

This is not uncommon. Half of the trauma that happens to us is either undiagnosed, unreported or we are unaware of it. And with the trauma that we are aware of and that is diagnosed, less than half of that is actually healed.[2] When you think about it, we are a society of trauma.

THE IMPACT OF TRAUMA

So, if we all have some sort of trauma in our pasts, what does it do to us? Well, it can, for example, lead to hypervigilance, whereby people search for problems in the future.[3] There are probably people in your life who seem to love a bit of drama, and it's easy to presume that they are just getting a kick out of it. Another client I worked with was a case in point. I initially thought she was someone who loved drama, but I soon realised that previous relationships had made her hypervigilant, and she was in some ways seeking conflict, not because she genuinely wanted it, but because she was trying to pre-empt it and therefore manage it.

Past trauma can also lead to deep-seated feelings of anxiety so that, when you're in a relationship, your partner can say something or do something that is perfectly natural to them, but that behaviour acts as a trigger for something that's happened in your past that you were unaware of. And then you get the ick, as some people say.

This is where I think mindset comes in. The psychologist Carol Dweck argues that we all have an open or closed mindset.[4] The latter is a sense that our skills and abilities are fixed, and, as a consequence, so too are our opportunities to grow. An open or growth mindset, on the other hand, is the belief that our skills and abilities are not fixed, and that we are on a journey on which we can learn and improve. Trauma, hypervigilance, anxiousness, avoidance — all of these things can contribute to creating or reinforcing a fixed mindset, whereas a sense that we can learn from the trauma in our past can lead us towards an open mindset, which allows us to better connect with people and be less neurotic in our relationships.

An open mindset is most obviously aligned with a secure attachment style and an absence of trauma. But trauma can also drive you to succeed, as it can be a motivating factor to learn and grow. And motivation is one of the three factors needed to convince us that we can change, the other two being inspiration and instruction.

Inspiration is having seen someone do it ahead of you, motivation is having a 'why' and instruction is someone laying out the blueprint for you. If we have the inspiration of knowing someone who has overcome something similar, the instruction of how to work through our problems and the motivation to make the change, we can use our past trauma to our advantage. These three things lead to an open mindset. When you don't have one of those things, you are likely to have less belief that you have any control of the situation, which lends itself to a fixed mindset.

Regardless of whether the trauma in your past has led you to have more of a fixed mindset, there is always a way to change your perspective. Even just picking up this book and starting to read it could open a crack in the door to a more open mindset. The instruction in this book begets the motivation which begets the inspiration. Or the inspiration begets the instruction which begets the motivation. Finding one can lead you to the next.

Once you've cracked open the door a little bit and have started to change your mindset, particularly around relationships and being open to the possibility of finding a partner in the future, there might still be some challenges along the way. In order to navigate those, you have to commit to being a lifelong learner and always striving to become a better person. The rewards if you do this are abundant. You're going to increase your chances of finding the right partner in the first place. You're going to be able to better communicate and have a stronger relationship with that partner. You're going to get closer to the point of self-actualisation (see page 12). If you have a family, your children are going to have better relationship skills. You're going to be able to use the skills you learn at work and within your village. Becoming a lifelong learner is just going to pay dividend after dividend after dividend.

THE BENEFITS OF THERAPY AND SELF-HEALING

Ultimately, the best way to deal with trauma is therapy, but it's not foolproof — less than half of the people who enter therapy find it to be helpful for them.[5] Also, in places like the UK, there's a massive shortage of therapists, it can be very expensive and there can be a long wait to see one. This is why it is also helpful to be able to self-heal. To me, therapy simply means healing, and you don't have to see a professional to be healed, although it is something that I advocate for.

There are also a lot of different types of therapy, but the idea in most cases is to first acknowledge and identify what happened and then begin to dissect it. To do that outside of a clinical environment, you can instead sit down with your village and begin to look at the relationships you have had and think about what happened and, most importantly, how those people showed you love. What did it look like? What did it feel like? When you felt pain, could you go to that person for emotional or physical comfort? Could you go to that person consistently? Or was that person not available to you all of the time? Did that person sometimes shun you? These basic questions will help you to understand how your past relationships shape who you are now and what your current attachment style is. And you can also use the questions in the table in Chapter 1 (page 23) to help you reflect a bit more on what your or your potential partner's attachment style might be.

Before I asked myself these types of questions, I presumed I had a secure attachment style, because my parents were great and I was brought up in a loving household. But when I really thought about it, I realised it wasn't as simple as that. My mother is first-generation Jamaican, my father is the first in his family to go to college, and they both worked long hours. As a result, I had a babysitter who was my main point of contact a lot of the time and, although I liked her, I sometimes didn't feel as if I could bring all of my issues to her, which must have also had an influence on my attachment style. That's why it's important to think about who you had in your life when you were growing up and how they showed you love and who you were able to go to to feel safe.

You also want to think about how those people experienced love. Who did your mother and father have in their lives? Who could they go to? Did they suffer any trauma? What was that trauma? Did they work through it? If yes, how? If not, is it possible that they're carrying that trauma with them to this day?

Recognising the trauma your parents experienced can shed light on certain patterns or behaviours within your family and help you to understand why your parents might have had specific emotional reactions, coping mechanisms or relationship dynamics. This understanding can foster empathy and compassion, and provide a broader context for family interactions. As I discussed previously, unaddressed trauma can be passed down through generations, creating a cycle of pain and dysfunction, so by identifying the trauma in your parents' lives, you can gain insight into how it might have influenced your upbringing and affected your own well-being. This awareness empowers you to break the cycle, make conscious choices, and engage in healing practices to promote your own mental and emotional health. In this way, recognising your parents' trauma can also be a vital part of your own healing journey. It can help you to understand any intergenerational effects that might have impacted you and provide an opportunity to address unresolved emotions or wounds stemming from your family history. This self-awareness can allow you to seek appropriate support, engage in therapeutic interventions and develop healthier coping strategies. Openly discussing and acknowledging the trauma in your parents' lives can also create opportunities for dialogue, healing and the strengthening of family bonds, promoting a culture of understanding, compassion and support within the family unit.

Once you've explored these concepts and where you might fit within the framework of attachment, and you've identified the potential trauma in your and your loved ones' lives, you can name it and begin to replace the negative emotions with positive ones. And that's where the healing occurs.

To help in this process, there's a long list of things you can turn to. Dr Gabor Maté's work is particularly helpful here, as he has identified a number of techniques that can help you to process trauma. For instance, cultivating mindfulness and engaging in meditation practices can help individuals develop self-awareness and increase their capacity to regulate emotions, as these techniques promote present-moment awareness, grounding and self-compassion. He also emphasises the importance of Compassionate Inquiry, a process that involves exploring and understanding the underlying causes and emotions related to trauma. This technique encourages individuals to approach their traumatic experiences with curiosity, empathy and non-judgement, creating a safe space for healing and self-discovery. Then there is connection and social support. Building strong, supportive relationships and finding a sense of community is vital for trauma healing, as is healthy emotional expression. In a more formal setting, Dr Maté highlights the significance of trauma-informed therapy approaches, such as eye movement desensitisation and reprocessing, somatic experiencing, and internal family systems. These therapies aim to address trauma on a physiological, emotional and cognitive level, facilitating healing and integration, and can be investigated further with qualified professionals.[6]

You can also begin to be healed through yoga therapy, art therapy, prayer, volunteer work, writing, journalling, gratitude exercises and workshops, reading books, talking to friends and family, watching YouTube videos . . . the list goes on — as we become more aware of the importance of looking after our mental health, the more resources there are available to us. All of these are methods to help you find joy and replace negative emotion with positive emotion. It's the same thing as forgiveness; it's just self-forgiveness.

Let's go back to that grandson I was talking about. When he was on a date, his first reaction when a woman asked him for something was that she wanted to use him for his money. But if he had done the work and begun to self-heal, he might have been able to recognise that as being something that triggered him. And once he'd recognised that, he might have been able to reframe his trauma. Instead of automatically flipping out when someone asked him for something, he'd have been able to say to himself, 'Hold on a second. Maybe they're not trying to use me.'

The village you surround yourself with is also important here. The healthier the relationships are in all aspects of your life, the better you can deal with your romantic relationships. And you can take a lead from the way that the people you know deal with stressful situations. Perhaps you know someone who seems to be able to bounce back quickly from a traumatic experience and operate with a cool head and without neuroticism. When something stressful happens to you, you can talk to that friend and take their advice. Multiple interactions like that will help to balance you out a little bit. Then when something stressful happens in your romantic relationship, you're less neurotic about it. In this way, the friends and family in your village can help you to self-heal too.

But it's also important to say that it's a process, and it takes a significant amount of time and active work. You also have to be aware of it, and most people are not aware. And not only are most people not aware, most people don't know what the work is that they need to do. And then they're not motivated enough to sustain that work.

Importantly, this is work that you can do outside of a relationship. In fact, as we touched on in the last chapter, before thinking about trying to find an ideal partner, it is beneficial to identify the trauma you've experienced, recognise your attachment style and begin to self-heal. You can of course become too focused on trauma and things that have gone wrong, and not enough on what makes you great and where your strengths lie and the good things that have happened, so there has to be a balance. And this is where self-compassion comes in — saying to yourself, 'I'm meant to be where I am.' There's so much value in accepting that you're enough. There's similar value in being imperfect and saying, 'Let me do the work. Let me start that process. And let me understand that by doing the work I'm not doing it in order to find a partner. I'm doing the work because I want to be my best self.' That's a very important part of relationships — ultimately, what you're trying to do is enhance your well-being and become your best self. And although you can have people who stimulate you and help you to get there, it's a personal journey.

GENERATIONAL AND CULTURAL DIFFERENCES

At Tinder, we publish a report called *The Future of Dating* every year.[7] Generation Z makes up roughly 50 per cent of the users of the app, so a lot of the focus is on that generation — with the eldest Gen Zers being about twenty-eight, they now make up the majority of the dating pool. They are the twenty-somethings who are out there actually meeting people. Whereas Gen Z grew up on apps, Gen X were the last generation to still have analogue, and if you talk to those of them who are single, they say things like, 'Why can't we meet somebody offline? That's how my parents and aunts and uncles met.'

In addition to generational differences, specific cultures are changing too — for example, African American culture, which is historically very conservative and highly church-based. If you speak to any Gen X or older Black American, I guarantee you, if they are single, someone in their family has said to them, 'Go to the church, baby, and find yourself a good one.' But when you talk to most Gen Z African Americans, they say, 'We haven't been to church in our life.'

The research that has been done on the Gen Z cohort tends to describe them as being pessimistic. They're also generally thought to be lonelier and have more mental health issues than any other generation. But I actually find them to be realists rather than pessimists. They're looking at the world and saying that there are a lot of crappy things happening out there. And they're being real by, for example, not wanting to have children because they are not optimistic about where we are headed. They're being real and they're being aware.

There is a lot of doom and gloom in the relationship landscape, but it's important to strike a balance between 'let's be real' and 'things are difficult'. Generally speaking, Gen Zers are aware of the trauma in their lives, and that this impacts their relationships, and that the person they're dating could have had traumatic events in their lives too. And so Gen Z, in my opinion, is the most authentic generation when it comes to dating.

What used to happen was someone would let you meet their representative to begin with. The representatives would negotiate and then, three months or so later, the real people would meet. With Gen Z, you're no longer meeting their representative. You're meeting someone who says, 'Look, I'm imperfect, and I know you're imperfect, so let's just put that on the table and begin there.'

The idea that there's only one partner out there for you and that fate will decide if you meet them echoes the fixed mindset that I mentioned earlier and the belief that you are on a predetermined path and can't change direction, whereas an open mindset tells you that there are multiple paths you can take and multiple partners out there who would be right for you. For this reason, I've never been one to believe that soulmates are found — I think soulmates are made. And this seems to tally with what the research is saying about Gen Z, which tends to be more open-minded and ready to accept differences and imperfections, and that there is no one perfect person out there for them. This is not the case for millennials, Gen Xers or baby boomers. Many of us have been brought up to believe that there is only one person for us because that idea has been beaten into us by society.

TRUSTWORTHY SOURCES OF RELATIONSHIP ADVICE

Our relationship IQ is higher than it's ever been, hence why I think Gen Zers better understand that there are multiple paths and soulmates out there for them. One of the conduits for us having a higher relationship IQ than we've ever had before is because relationships and love are such a big part of our culture today. We spend a lot of time watching romcoms and dating shows, and reading about love in magazines. But the biggest reason is that we've never had as much data and research available to us as we do today. We have more people studying mating psychology than ever before, and we have major institutions like Tinder, which has created more than 75 billion matches, that are able to study people's professed desires but also their behaviours. Who are people actually clicking on? This data informs apps like Tinder and then enters society through television, through social media, through films. And that's why we have participants on dating shows talking about attachment theory.

But all of this information is both a gift and a curse. For example, the algorithms on social media serve you up what is controversial, because it is the people who have the extreme views who are able to make themselves heard above all of the noise. The points of view that they are putting forward are the ones that then become popular on TikTok or Instagram, and those are the things that are brought into the household, or the barbershop, or the playground, or the workplace, and discussed, even if we are not in a position to fully understand the information.

This harks back to what I was talking about in the Introduction. On the one side you've got all the psychologists and the biologists and the psychiatrists who have done the research — let's call them the empirical group. They talk a certain lingo, and they're basically writing reports for each other. On the other side you have the laypeople who are relying on incomplete information based on the experiences of non-experts — let's call them the anecdotal group, which is much bigger. The empirical group is not really sharing their information in a way that makes it accessible or easy to understand, even though we have at least twenty to thirty years of hardcore data that would answer a lot of the questions that the anecdotal group have.

A simple example would be: should straight women approach straight men? The anecdotal group debates this question constantly — it's probably a top-ten debate, even as society has become more progressive overall — and I think the lion's share of people still come down on the side of saying that a woman should never approach a man. But the data shows us that the number-one issue men have in connecting with women is the fear of approaching them and being rejected. So, most men would love it if a woman approached them. It shouldn't even be a debate, but it is because there's a lot of noise in the anecdotal group, based around learned behaviour from limited experiences and what people are reading in magazines or watching on dating programmes rather than what the data is actually telling us.

I discuss all things relationships on a weekly segment on *Lorraine*. A while ago, two people came up to me when I was on holiday and said, 'Paul, we watch you on *Lorraine*, and it's like our counselling session. We use the advice you give in our relationships.' And it really hit me that, for the vast majority of people, television and social media is their only source of information when it comes to relationships. It baffles me that I spent a full year learning trigonometry in high school, and I've not used it once, but I was taught more or less nothing about relationships, even though that would have been a valuable life skill to learn.

Today, we live online, where it's the people who shout the loudest who cut through the noise, but, as I mentioned, they don't necessarily have the best messages. So, how do we find the more positive instructional voices that are worth listening to? After all, we can't ignore social content, and we can't ignore TV.

My general philosophy is that the best advice comes from someone who matches your values. If you're getting instruction from someone who doesn't match your values and who lives their life to a different set of rules, what they say or do might not necessarily apply to you. It's also important to get relationship advice from people who have theoretical as well as practical experience. Some people don't have either — they just have opinions — and they should be avoided too. And last but not least, it's important to know that the person you're getting the advice from is walking their talk. If a person is doing that and has practical and theoretical knowledge while also sharing your values, they are in a position to give you advice that is usable. And it is your responsibility to go after that by following and engaging with people who meet those criteria. The algorithms are not going to serve you that. You have to go after something deeper.

In his book *Friends*, Robin Dunbar includes a lot of data to suggest that our social circles are shrinking and have been doing so for years.[8] And, unfortunately, as we get older, our social circles tend to shrink anyway. Think back to the men who now have no 3am friends. This is extremely dangerous. There is strong evidence to suggest that the value of a village is great, but it's not just about any group of people. It's about a group of people who you know, who share your values and who are supportive. You need a strong group of friends, a strong village, to access this deeper source of relationship advice.

It's not about getting one person's opinion. It's about consensus. And it's about people guiding you to come up with the answers yourself. This is only possible if you give them unbiased information. My father and brother are both computer engineers, and they always say, 'Bad data in, bad data out.' The key is you serving your village information in as unbiased a way as possible, and then allowing them to give you feedback and you taking the consensus of that feedback. You get rational thought from a strong group of peers.

And in order to remove the bias — to put good data in and get good data back — you have to know yourself, and you have to do the work. You have to acknowledge the trauma and heal, and it's only when you get to that place that you can start to navigate the noise and find the signal.

KEY TAKEAWAYS

1. Recognising and dealing with the past trauma in your life, romantic or otherwise, is necessary before you look for love.

2. Soulmates are made not found, and there are multiple potential partners out there for you.

3. We are strongly influenced by culture and our emotions when looking for a partner, but we should instead be relying more on the data from psychology and relationship science.

'IF YOU WANT A SUCCESSFUL LONG-TERM RELATIONSHIP, YOU FIRST HAVE TO BUILD A STRONG SENSE OF SELF AND BE COMFORTABLE WITH WHO YOU ARE, WHY YOU ARE AND HOW YOU SHOW UP'

3

A STRONG SENSE OF SELF IS THE KEY TO A SUCCESSFUL RELATIONSHIP

If the last chapter advocated for the benefits of a type of self-reflection based around looking to your past and examining the cultural forces that shape your relationship searches, this one continues that process but shifts the focus even closer to home by asking you to consider whether you are satisfied with your own life and encouraging you to think about what your values and goals are before you try to find love.

If you want a successful long-term relationship, you first have to build a strong sense of self and be comfortable with who you are, why you are and how you show up. You often hear people say, 'You gotta love yourself first.' In essence, what they're really saying is that you need to have a strong sense of self: 'I know who I am, and I like who I am.'

Being happy with your own life and who you are before you start to seek a relationship or a partner can be easier said than done, of course, as a lot of people find it challenging to determine whether they are happy. This is where psychology can help us, because investigating what makes people happy, or satisfied, has become an increasingly important field of research since about the 1980s, culminating in Martin Seligman coining the term 'positive psychology' in the late 1990s.[1]

However, instead of referring to happiness, psychologists tend to talk about subjective well-being. This is generally measured by asking people to self-report by answering questionnaires that ask things such as: am I happy with life as a whole? Am I satisfied with the relationships I have with my friends and family? Do I feel fulfilled and satisfied with my career or work? Am I satisfied with my physical health?[2] Sometimes the questions require a yes or no answer, like these ones, whereas others, like in the *World Happiness Report*,[3] ask their respondents to grade their life satisfaction on a scale.

Even more useful is the six-factor model of psychological well-being (PWB) developed by Carol Ryff. This assessment tool measures six dimensions of well-being:

autonomy, environmental mastery, personal growth, positive relations with others, purpose in life and self-acceptance. High scores in each of these areas points to someone who is psychologically healthy and leading a good life. It is, in essence, a way of quantifiably measuring if someone is on the path to self-actualisation and being the best version of themselves.[4]

Doing one of these assessments can be a useful way of ascertaining whether you are happy and fulfilled now, but I think the key thing is working out whether you are on the path to becoming happy and fulfilled. If the answer to that is yes, then you're more likely to be satisfied with your lot. But why is that important? Well, when you feel happy and fulfilled, you are more likely to attract someone and engage in a relationship with someone who's also happy and fulfilled.

HIGH SELF-SATISFACTION LEADS TO STRONGER RELATIONSHIPS

Having higher self-satisfaction is really one of the secrets to having strong satisfaction in your partnership. Now that we expect more from our relationships, a high level of personal satisfaction in your life generally can help contribute to a higher level of satisfaction within your partnership.[5] And it works both ways. Robert Walding-er's book *The Good Life* is partly informed by his work on the Harvard Study of Adult Development, which has been running for more than seventy-five years. In his research, he has found that the stronger the relation-ships you have — and we're talking quality here rather than quantity — the better your life becomes. You live longer, you're healthier and you're happier. When he tried to work out why this might be the case, the answer he came up with was that those strong relationships dra-matically improve your well-being and help you to manage stress.[6] In fact, people who have stronger rela-tionships have lower levels of cortisol, which is considered to be one of the most significant of the so-called stress hormones. In modern life, we all have to deal with lots of stress every day, so if we don't have those meaningful connections, we are missing out on an invaluable resource to help us manage it.

The lower your self-satisfaction before you enter a relationship, the higher your stress levels and the harder it will be to make that relationship a success. The separa-tion rates for these people are higher than for people who come into a relationship with personal fulfilment.[7] It makes sense, right? Because it's going to be more chal-lenging earlier on in your relationship. Every couple needs to work on their relationship, striving for stronger communication, higher life satisfaction, better sex, and the hope is that the satisfaction of your relationship will grow over time. But if you enter a relationship from a place of strength it can become even stronger. This is why Eli Finkel's work has shown that the most satisfied marriages of today are happier than they ever have been in the history of recorded marriage.[8] It's as a result of understanding and doing the work and coming in strong.

If you don't do the work on yourself before looking for someone, instead of choosing a partner with clarity, you're probably not even choosing a partner — you're probably being chosen. I think that happens a lot, and, unfortunately, it happens more often to women. If you don't have a strong sense of self, you have no idea who you are and what you stand for, and you're therefore most likely to be chosen by one of the dark-tetrad personality types: a narcissist, a Machiavellian, a psychopath or a sadist (more of which in Chapter 8). And you're more likely to become co-dependent on the relationship and on your partner.

When it comes to actually selecting a partner, being happy and fulfilled helps you to be more intentional and thoughtful in the choices that you're making, because it means you're not making your decisions based on fear. When you make choices based on fear, rather than from a position of empowerment and being fulfilled, you're not optimising your ability to make those decisions.

I mentioned before that studies we have done at Tinder show that the main reason why men are not in relationships is fear of rejection. But we're only born with two fears: falling and loud noises.[9] Every other fear that we have, whether that's public speaking or talking to someone for the first time, is learned. We basically grow up and freak ourselves out, and by doing so we minimise the effectiveness of our decisions. This is because our flight response kicks in when we make a decision in a state of fear. We essentially turn our backs on the scenario and are no longer thinking rationally about what's happening in the moment. All we're thinking about is how to minimise our fear. When we make decisions like this, we're also less willing to take risks, and that's where the opportunities are. That's where the growth is.

In addition, it's worth thinking about some of the behaviours that accompany fear. You're probably speaking more quickly. You might look a bit erratic. You could be sweating. This means that, when you're in a state of fear, whoever you're interacting with is reading that you can't be trusted. That you're not someone they can believe in. You're already putting yourself on the back foot.

THINGS TO WORK ON BEFORE YOU MEET YOUR PARTNER

So, what aspects of your life should you be content with before embarking on a relationship? We've already talked a bit about self-esteem, but low neuroticism is also very important. If something emotionally challenging happens in your life — you lose a job or a close family member passes away — how quickly do you bounce back? Those who are lower on the neurotic scale are able to rebound from adversity more easily, and they're better partners too. Closely related to this is emotional stability, as it also contributes to your resilience and ability to recover from adversity. And it's this emotional stability that makes us great partners. When you're emotionally stable, you are better able to resolve conflict and provide emotional support to your loved one (more on this in Chapter 7).

Next is looking at your career and personal goals. I hate it when I hear people say, especially for men, 'You have to have your dream job before you're married.' I don't believe that's true, but I do believe society has wrapped our careers into our identities. When I meet new people, they typically talk about what they do before they talk about who they are. And quite often when very successful people retire, they lose their sense of purpose. So, while I don't think your career should be the be-all and end-all, it is important to have career and personal goals — the most satisfied people are those who have goals, even if they're retired. Even more importantly, do you feel like you're on the pathway to reaching those goals?

It is also extremely worthwhile to spend a bit of time assessing your friendships and social circles. You don't have to have a massive group of friends, but a small group of high-quality relationships is so beneficial. To this end, ask yourself whether you have any of those 3am friends. If you don't, why do you think that is, and can you do more to bond with people on a platonic level? It's such an important aspect of ensuring you are nurtured.

Again, having a village of supportive people around you is vital, as it's your community before you enter your relationship that allows you to feel fulfilled. This helps us to avoid the chicken-and-egg situation of on the one hand needing to be fulfilled to find a healthy relationship, but a healthy relationship being one of the most important factors in us feeling fulfilled. The answer is that it's not just romantic relationships we're talking about — you need to have that village, that community, prior to even looking for a romantic relationship.

You should have also figured out how to engage in healthy relationships before you embark on the search for a long-term partner. The people around you can help you to learn how to communicate and set boundaries. Your village is like the training ground before you get to the World Cup. And it's a virtuous circle, because once you do end up in a healthy romantic relationship, it helps sustain your satisfaction and sense of fulfilment. And there's a snowball effect if you choose to have children further down the line. They start at a graduated level because they've seen what a healthy relationship looks like, which in turn makes it more likely that they will have a secure attachment style, and helps avoid the kind of intergenerational trauma we talked about in the previous chapter. The question of who you go out on a date with tonight is a decision that could end up impacting not just your life, but the lives of those who come after you.

Last but not least are your values, which I view as being the enduring beliefs and principles that individuals hold, and which guide their attitudes, behaviours and decision-making processes. In other words, values are the guiding frameworks that shape individuals' preferences, priorities and actions in various aspects of their lives, including their relationships. Individuals prioritising similar values have higher relationship satisfaction and compatibility because shared primary values create a sense of alignment and understanding between partners.[10]

It is your values and the other information you know about yourself, including the trauma in your past and your attachment style, that help you to work out what your relationship goals are. And the journey to choosing a partner can only really happen once you've selected those relationship goals, which are essentially just ways of quantifying more precisely what it is that you want from love.

So, do you have a rulebook for life? I believe that if you have identified your top values, and you're feeding them on a consistent basis, that will increase your self-esteem. For example, my top values are family, creativity and ambition, and I'm constantly trying to pay attention to and prioritise those things. I always say I'm working to save money so I can travel with my family. That's my life. The more time I spend feeding my values of family, creativity and ambition, the more satisfied I am with me, and the higher my self-esteem is. And this is relevant from a dating perspective, because when you're fulfilled, you have more clarity when it comes to partner selection, as you're better able to identify their values and whether they align with yours.

CHAPTER 3

SETTING RELATIONSHIP GOALS

Once you've taken the time to assess your life satisfaction and identify your values, the next step in preparing yourself to find love is to set your relationship goals and define what it is you are looking for in a relationship and from a partner.

Over the last couple of years, people have begun to talk about 'situationships' — in other words, relationships without clearly defined goals or boundaries. And while that might work for you in the moment, entering a relationship with no clear sense of what you want from it is going to make it difficult for it to be a success. In response to this, dating apps like Tinder introduced the relationship goals feature that we discussed in Chapter 1. This is key because most of us enter a relationship without having identified what we truly want, and that's why we're accepting of what we don't need — of what the other person puts on us.

Say you go on a date with someone and they say, 'I'm not looking for anything serious right now.' Nine times out of ten, if you're physically attracted to them and the date is going well, the conversation is flowing and you're having a good time, your response is going to be, 'Yeah, me too,' even if you are actually looking for something long-term.

And then what ends up happening is you go on another date, and another date, and another date, and they've already made it clear that they just want short-term, but you want long-term — now you're in a situationship.

This has become more of a problem as dating has evolved over the years. Remember, dating in the past was just a one-way street to marriage. That was it. But now there a million different outcomes, so ending up in a situationship is much more likely if you don't set out your goals to begin with. Being crystal clear on what you want is key. And to work that out, you need to look at your core beliefs and values. Going back to my values, family is very high on my list, so a short-term relationship probably wouldn't have been right for me.

You also need to work out what your long-term aspirations are in life, and really think about how a relationship could support or enhance those goals. And to me that's not about being hypergamous (looking for someone who has the same or greater level of status than you) or a gold-digger or anything along those lines. Instead, what you're saying is, 'I'm looking for a partner in life, so how do my goals align with that partner?' Maybe your long-term goal is to not have a home base and to travel the world and be a nomad. So you need to find someone who wants to do that too.

Next, ask yourself what your personal strengths and areas for growth are, and think about how a partner could support or challenge you in those areas. Iron sharpens iron, so you need a partner who is going to help you become your best self, not hold you back or limit your potential in any way.

Then there are what I call my non-starters — other people might say deal-breakers or non-negotiables (I go into these red flags in more detail in Chapter 8). These are anything that directly impact your health or happiness. If a person does something that negatively affects you, why even engage with them?

COMMUNICATION STYLES

It is also useful to be aware of what type of communication style works best for you. There are many different names for communication styles, but the most clear and helpful definitions I have found are: direct, indirect, open, avoidant and passive-aggressive.

DIRECT

A direct communication style involves clear and explicit expression of thoughts, feelings and needs. Individuals who use direct communication tend to be straightforward, honest and assertive in expressing themselves, which can contribute to effective problem-solving and understanding in relationships.

INDIRECT

Indirect communication refers to the expression of thoughts, feelings or needs in a subtle or implicit manner. This might involve hinting, using non-verbal cues or relying on context to convey messages. Indirect communicators often value harmony and avoid direct confrontation, but it can lead to misunderstandings or unmet needs if not effectively understood by their partners.

OPEN

Open communication involves a willingness to share thoughts, emotions and experiences with a partner. Individuals who engage in open communication are comfortable expressing vulnerability, discussing sensitive topics and actively listening to their partners. Open communication fosters trust, intimacy and a deeper understanding of each other's perspectives.

AVOIDANT

The opposite of open communication, avoidant communication involves the tendency to evade or avoid discussing sensitive or difficult topics. Individuals using avoidant communication have a tendency to withdraw, change the subject, or use distractions to avoid confronting conflict or uncomfortable issues. This style can hinder problem-solving and emotional connection in relationships.

PASSIVE-AGGRESSIVE

Passive-aggressive communication is similar in some ways to indirect communication, but it might also involve sarcasm, backhanded compliments, or non-verbal cues that convey hostility or resistance. Passive-aggressive communication can lead to misunderstandings and undermine relationship satisfaction if the underlying issues are not addressed openly.[11]

In my experience, people rarely think about communication when they're entering a relationship, but it's very important, because it is the lifeblood of a partnership. That's why you need to think about what your communication style is and what sort of communication you want from someone else.

Sometimes one person in a relationship has stronger goals or pursues them more energetically, and as a result you could end up with a power imbalance if you're not careful. This is where the other pieces come into play. You have to be able to negotiate using good communication. You have to establish your core values at the outset. You have to make clear and advocate for your long-term goals and aspirations. And you have to stand by your need for personal growth (one of Ryff's six dimensions of PWB).

Yes, you want someone to stretch you, and you want to be placed in scenarios that are outside of your comfort zone to help you grow, but you also want to make sure that you are not made to do something you don't want to do. This touches upon satisfaction and co-dependency again. If you don't have high life satisfaction, you could easily find yourself obliging a person who said, for example, 'Let's travel the world,' because, if you're unhappy, you might think what they are suggesting is going to fix things. They move you to Thailand, but you don't like it, and they sense that you're miserable, so they fall in love with someone else. Now you're stuck somewhere you didn't even want to be in the first place. And all of this could have been avoided if you had been clearer with yourself, and your partner, about what you really wanted.

If you know your values and are on the pathway to fulfilment, that's going to allow you to articulate what your relationship goals are more clearly. And you can then lean on your village for support and guidance. As

I said, the people around you can increase your life satisfaction and teach you the skills you need: communication, self-awareness, boundary-setting, and so on. Or maybe someone in your village is doing something incredible that you find inspirational. Maybe you are motivated by your friends and family, or perhaps they can offer you insight and instruction.

In her book *Generations*, Dr Jean Twenge says that one of the main reasons Gen Z is the most different from all the other cohorts is because it's fully digital, and Gen Zers are no longer having as many face-to-face conversations.[12] The issue with everything being online, and especially if you spend a lot of time on social media, is that you're no longer getting a slice of reality — you're getting a highlight reel that you can never truly aspire to. The inevitable reaction to this, one informed by fear, is that you feel you can't match up. As a result, Gen Z has the highest instances of mental illness and loneliness. So just having a face-to-face conversation with someone in your village who you trust is tremendously beneficial when you are looking for a partner.

I already mentioned that fear can block us from making logical decisions. Now some of you might say that love is not logical, it's an emotion, but I think the pursuit of love is very logical. It's like if you want to play a professional sport – you need to have incredible skill and talent, but you also have to practise and put yourself in the best position to succeed. Even if you do the extra things you need to do, you might still not make it, but you definitely won't if you just rely on your talent. Love is similar – you need to put yourself in the best position to find a partner who is right for you. There are no guarantees, but if you do the work, there's a greater chance that you will end up in a strong relationship.

Marriage and long-term relationships are not for everyone, but I also don't think that we're meant to be on earth alone. We're social creatures. And I truly believe that if you are doing this work on yourself, and your desire is to be in a relationship, no matter what type of relationship that is, then you will eventually be successful. The road to this point feels very logical.

Every time someone says to me, 'All these guys out here suck!' or 'All the women out here are terrible. I've done everything right. Why am I still single?' and I sit down and unpack their dating history, I inevitably discover that they haven't done the work on themselves to maximise their chances of success. Let me give you an example. I had a client here in the UK who was in her early fifties who said to me, 'I've been online for six months, and I attract almost no men, but the men I do attract are complete arseholes. They are the worst of the worst. They're terrible. Men just suck.' So I said, 'Take a couple of photos of your profile and send them to me. Maybe I can give you some input.' Her profile consisted of a photo, her name, her age and a bio that basically said that all the men she met online were crazy people and she only wanted to receive messages from people who were sane. She was screaming out, 'I have trust issues. I am not satisfied with my life. I am disgruntled.' The work that she needed to do on herself was so apparent, but she was quick to place the blame elsewhere. That's an issue a lot of us have: we're quick to point the finger — at other people, at social media, at dating sites — but we are rarely willing to be self-reflective and do the work.

It may of course be that you are not in the best place personally when an opportunity to connect with a suitable partner presents itself. In those situations, you just need to start where you are, but you are going to be at a bit of a disadvantage. It's like running a race. It's better to have bought a great pair of running shoes and have a water bottle in your hand before you get started. You could of course go back to the starting line to pick those things up if you wanted to, and you'd still be in the race, but you'd be behind.

In relationship terms, if you go back and do the work on yourself once you've already chosen a partner, further down the line you might find that you're not happy in life, your values don't align, you have different goals and you shouldn't have been in the relationship at all. It's far better to have started the work ahead of time.

And all of this is a lifelong process. As I said before, you don't have to be at the destination of self-actualisation and high psychological well-being to find your perfect partner, but you do have to be on the path, and you do have to engage proactively in the process, taking logical steps towards fulfilling your emotional needs. So make sure you prioritise your own happiness and well-being before trying to find the love of your life, and take the time to work out what your values and goals are. The rewards now and in the future will be plentiful.

KEY TAKEAWAYS

1. Being happy and having a strong sense of self are necessary if you want to have a successful long-term relationship.

2. Stronger relationships lead to you being happier and healthier, as they help you to lower and manage stress.

3. Being happy and fulfilled means you are less likely to make decisions based on fear, and you can select the right partner for you, rather than allowing yourself to be chosen.

'ONCE YOU'VE DONE ALL
OF THE WORK ON
YOURSELF, PAST AND
PRESENT, YOU THEN HAVE
TO LOOK AT THE LANDSCAPE
AND IDENTIFY THE PATH
YOU'RE GOING TO TAKE TO
THE SUMMIT'

4

HOW YOUR ENVIRONMENT SHAPES YOUR SEARCH FOR A PARTNER

The first thing I do every morning before I walk my boys to school is ask Siri what the weather is like that day. I'm checking the environment so that I know what to wear and what to take — do I need a coat or an umbrella? Also, if it's going to rain, we take a different path, because I know our regular one is liable to flood. By checking my environment, it helps to dictate the route that I take. And that's just when I'm taking my kids to school. Looking for a long-term partner is more akin to trying to reach the top of the mountain — failing to check the environment before you embark on such an expedition could lead to disaster.

In my experience, people talk a lot about how finding a partner is down to chance. And to an extent, they might be right, but I strongly believe that you can manage that chance and increase the likelihood that you're going to find someone by looking at the whole equation. In this chapter we are going to look at a piece of the equation that virtually no one spends time thinking about when they're searching for a partner. And that is the environment in which you are trying to find love. Once you've done all of the work on yourself, past and present, you then have to look at the landscape and identify the path you're going to take to the summit. From a strategic point of view, if you can better understand the environment, you can increase your chances of finding the right person.

When I refer to 'environment' in a dating context, I mean a couple of things: the first is the influence that the hidden force of evolution has on human behaviour, and the second is the world in which we look for love today. Together they create the playing field that we operate within. Although seemingly quite different, they are both forces that are largely outside of our control, hence why I think of them as being environmental factors. But just because they are out of our control does not mean that there is no value in understanding them, as knowledge and awareness are power.

THE ROLE OF EVOLUTION

It is difficult to draw the dividing line between our cognitive inheritance and the agency that comes via socialisation — the nature/nurture debate is a long-standing one and seemingly no nearer to being resolved. And perhaps it doesn't even make sense to think of it as an either/or situation — instead, we might be better to think of it as a continuum, with different forces at play all at once. Nonetheless, knowing that there is a wired element to our preferences is valuable knowledge. There are behaviours that are not only happening inside us but within the people with whom we're seeking to enter relationships too, and this influences the environment in which we are operating.

In order to better understand human behaviour when it comes to relationships, evolutionary psychology has become the foundation that a lot of therapists use to explain why we act the way we do. How have we developed cognitively? Why are we attracted to certain attributes and put off by others? There has been some criticism of evolutionary psychology — for example, that it often doesn't include enough cultural aspects to it and that not enough work has been done to understand mating outside of straight relationships[1] — but there is also some phenomenal research being done, particularly when it comes to mating, by people like David Buss and colleagues in his lab at the University of Texas in Austin.

One of the biggest points of confusion when it comes to finding a partner is down to what evolutionary psychology would call short-term versus long-term mating. There's a different strategy if you're looking for sex tonight versus looking for a partner for life. You look for different characteristics. You behave differently. You play up certain traits and downplay others. That's the reason why the relationship goals that we talked about in the last chapter are so important (see page 77).

Evolutionary psychology shows us that women, regardless of sexual orientation, are more interested in long-term relationships on average.[2] And why is that? Well, the way our psychology evolved during our early development as a species was really driven by procreation. If a woman became pregnant, she would have to go at least nine months before she could conceive another child. In that time, it was to her advantage to have a partner to help to sustain her and her unborn child's lives. And when the child was born, it was to her advantage to continue to have a partner to protect her and her offspring. If you were a man and your mission was procreation, you could do that every day if you wanted to. There was no advantage to being in a long-term partnership as our early ancestors evolved.[3]

Some people will counter this by citing monogamous relationships in ancient cultures. In ancient Greece and ancient Rome, for example, men were only permitted to have one wife. However, in ancient Greece men would sleep with their slaves, and prostitution was encouraged in ancient Rome. Men have not evolved to be monogamous.[4]

So what persuaded men that it was worth pursuing monogamous relationships and having just one partner? There were a number of forces at play, but the most significant was the church. During the Carolingian dynasty of the eighth and ninth centuries CE, you had the rise of what we can call the Western Church. Prior to this, most of us lived in patriarchal clans and people would marry within that group — this often meant marrying a cousin — as it made sense to keep all of the resources within your clan. You didn't look up to God; you looked up to the patriarch of the clan or some sort of local symbol or idol. When the Western Church was trying to establish its foothold in central Europe, it used marriage and family to help disassemble the clan and replace the patriarch with God. To this end, it banned first cousins from marrying, which forced people to travel away from their homes to find a partner. The church also prevented illegitimate children from inheriting from their fathers, thereby penalising you for having extramarital offspring. Measures such as these led to the deconstruction of the clans into small, nuclear families. These individual families then began to opt into towns. And this led to the formation of societies with democratic structures that value and promote monogamy.

Despite the fact that monogamy was a construct imposed on us in large part by the church, there are other factors at play too. First, biology counters the urge for men to procreate. Testosterone levels are much higher in young, single men, and if you fall in love with someone, your testosterone levels drop.[5] Then, if you have children, your testosterone levels drop some more.[6] Why? Because there is an urge to keep things stable and avoid danger. Biologically, men are less prone to go out and cheat. We're also living in a day and age in which more of our needs are being met by our partners. Your partner is your best friend, your lover, co-CFO of the household finances and potentially a co-parent. And then there are the social and cultural aspects that promote the benefits of being in a stable relationship in the twenty-first century. Even today, there's a tremendous amount of negative stigma around cheating that keeps a lot of people monogamous.

Regardless of whether you are looking for a short- or long-term mate, or one partner or many, we have evolved to be attracted to how people look. This physical attractiveness is sometimes described in terms of the 'golden mean'. In women, this is generally thought to be a ratio of waist to hips of 70 per cent or less.[7] Throughout history, and across cultures, straight men, on average, have found this to be attractive. Now the question is why? How is it possible that there is a standard that goes across cultures and throughout history? Well, it's evolution again. In the early stages of our development, a woman with those measurements was thought to be optimally fertile, and this is what straight men typically sought — someone to help them further their legacy and sustain life through procreation. Even if you look at how tastes have changed over the years, the golden mean has endured. In the 1960s and 1970s, you had models like Twiggy who were slim but still conformed to the 70 per cent waist-to-hips ratio. In recent years, we've been going through a more voluptuous stage, typified by someone like Kim Kardashian, who took the golden mean to its extremes. So, this has always been attractive on average for straight men. It's just something that we have to own — it's built-in.

And there is a golden mean for what straight women find physically attractive in men too. For them, it is a man's shoulders and chest being wider than his waist. Why does this matter? Because it suggests that he's strong and able to protect her. If we return to hunter-gatherer days, a man's ability to fend off attackers meant life or death for a woman and her offspring. If you fast-forward to today and a woman says, 'I find a man that looks like that sexy,' it comes from somewhere. Part of our response to how we want our partners to look has been programmed over the years. But there are cultural aspects to this too, and that's where agency comes in. We still have personal preferences. For example, you could say that certain cultures and subcultures perhaps favour a slimmer or wider delta when it comes to those golden-mean measurements. And work is still being done to understand how these psychological forces play themselves out in the context of gay and lesbian preferences.

MATE VALUE

Related to physical attractiveness is mate value, another concept from evolutionary psychology. Outside of academia, this idea is quite controversial — 'Oh my God, you're assigning value to me like I'm some sort of object!' But it's just a way of naming and identifying a thing that many of us do when we say something like, 'He's an eight out of ten.' From an evolutionary psychology standpoint, 'mate value' is essentially the value that we bring to the mating market. In order to make yourself more compelling when it comes to finding love, you need to increase that value, which I also call 'social capital' (see Chapter 6). And you can do that in a number of ways, because your mate value is relative, and it's based on a variety of things: your attractiveness, your social status, whether or not you have children, where you come from and what you do for work. It also includes your mindset and how you show up in a room — for example, with confidence and curiosity. There are so many pieces that add up to give you your mate value.

If you can grasp that concept, you can then manage your mate value and better understand how people interpret it. Ultimately, managing your mate value means enhancing certain skills, showcasing your strongest qualities (for mating) and cultivating a fulfilling life. It's about knowing and owning that you are the star of your own life, as my friend and fellow matchmaker Maria Avgitidis Pyrgiotakis would put it.

Studies have shown that men generally assign themselves a higher mate value than they actually have, while women do the opposite.[8] This perception dramatically impacts how you show up in the dating marketplace and who you pursue. A straight man who perceives himself to have a high mate value is looking for a woman who's super attractive, intelligent and kind — basically, the greatest of all time. He's probably also more often than not looking for a long-term partner. A man who perceives himself to have a lower mate value is not looking for the most attractive woman and is interested in short-term, because he doesn't believe that he could sustain a long-term relationship. These two men go into the dating environment and operate differently based on these perceptions. On the flipside, it's also why so many women accept less than they want — they perceive themselves to have a lower mate value.

A lot of this happens without us really being aware of it — we just have a general sense of our value, which in turn informs what we will settle for. By trying to understand your mate value more accurately, you can begin to manage and improve it. The higher value you have, the more opportunities and options you have.

COGNITIVE BIASES

We are also generally unaware of the cognitive biases that influence our reactions and decision-making processes, even though they can play an important role when you are trying to find a partner. For example, confirmation bias is a huge one when it comes to dating. Perhaps you meet someone new and immediately assign them a low mate value — because when we are interacting with someone, we're inevitably assigning them a value in our heads — and from that point onwards, all you're looking to do is confirm the value that you've assigned. Maybe you say, 'This guy's a five out of ten at best,' and from then on you're looking for all of the characteristics that prove to you that he's only a five: 'Look how he's chewing his food!'

The halo effect is another bias that works to our disadvantage when it comes to dating. I also call this the pretty-girl or pretty-boy effect. You see someone who's attractive, so you think they're everything else too: they're kind, they're smart, they're generous ... But what someone looks like has no bearing whatsoever on what sort of person they are. Research shows that we also do this by association. If we meet someone and they are with someone else whom we think is attractive or has a high mate value, we are more likely to assign those same qualities to the first person.[9]

If you are aware of these biases, you can begin to manage and overcome them: 'Hold on a second. I'm falling into confirmation bias. Let me back up. He's eating chips like everybody else.' This is not to say that it's easy to overcome our biases — it's hard and can take an incredible amount of work. But the most important step, just like dealing with trauma, is to be aware that they exist. Awareness is key, because it helps us to better navigate our environment and informs how we interact with the people in it.

The silver lining is that everyone is a gift from heaven to someone. There is someone out there among the 8 billion people in the world to whom you would be a gift just the way you are. We are living in the most inclusive era in the history of this planet. And the beauty of that is more people are willing to date outside of their religion, or outside of their race, or outside of their geography. In other words, more people are open to everyone. And while physical attractiveness isn't off the menu, other traits are increasing in importance (see page 184).

So, if you can begin to work on your mate value and get your biases under control, you'll be able to widen the pool so that there are ten people out there, or a hundred, or a thousand, who would want to be with you. Yes, the paradox of choice can become a factor, so there's a delicate balance, but I believe you have to increase your chances of finding someone by appealing to more people.

You have to start by saying, 'I'm enough as I am. All I'm doing is widening the pool.'

SEX RATIO

Another term from evolutionary psychology that is relevant to the straight dating landscape is 'sex ratio', which is the number of men to every 100 women.* At the world population level, the ratio is approximately 101 men to 100 women, but this can fluctuate at a national level — like in China, for example, following their one-child policy — or within a local environment such as a university campus thanks to more women now enrolling in higher education than men.[10] Once there is an imbalance in the sex ratio in any given environment, we act differently. In China, the overabundance of men means that they have to compete with other men to attract the smaller group of women.[11] And on the flipside, the women can now demand more from the men, including insisting upon long-term relationships, because they have the leverage of a favourable sex ratio. If you look at college campuses, on the other hand, where you have an

---

* I have not yet seen any research on whether sex ratio is a factor in same-sex communities.

abundance of women and a smaller number of men, the men run wild. They have fewer committed relationships because they have negotiating power. As a result, we operate differently when we're in these environments without even realising it.

If you find yourself as a man or woman in a negative sex ratio — say you're a woman on a university campus where there's far fewer men to choose from — knowing this can be helpful. Marcus Garvey famously said, 'When man becomes possessor of the knowledge of himself, he becomes master of his environment.'[12] Once you're armed with that information, you can put yourself in a different environment. Or when you're in that environment and you have an understanding of the challenges it presents, you can change your behaviour and know what boundaries to hold. I think what happens, especially to a lot of straight women, is that they feel pressure to act in a certain way, because they assume that's what everyone is doing — for example, the woman on the campus thinks you have to sleep with lots of guys to find a partner. But once you have a general awareness that a negative sex ratio is in place, you can be more confident in maintaining your boundaries.

Culture also shapes the environment that you're in. Say you're a woman in Ghana on an engineering programme mainly made up of men. The concept of sex ratio would make you think that the woman would have a lot of control over what's happening. But you're in one of many countries around the world where patriarchal power structures still dominate, so there's going to be less of an impact there. It is also important to acknowledge here that a lot of data on this comes from the WEIRD nations, so some of this is less likely to apply in other places with different cultural norms.

In the West, social media plays a significant role in shaping those societal norms. If you look at every generation above Gen Z, the content that they consumed was created by an older generation. When I was growing up as a Gen Xer and watching Saturday cartoons, it was most likely someone from my parents' generation who had made them. Gen Z is the first generation to start consuming content not made predominantly by the older generations but by itself. And this has a huge impact on what Gen Zers perceive to be societal norms, sometimes positively but largely negatively. Getting information from peers is positive because the information tends to be more accessible and people therefore pay more attention to it, and the fact that it's a peer delivering it tends to make it relatable. The issue, though, is that a peer will have less life experience (on average) compared to someone from an older generation. Also, advice from within your own cohort can be influenced by groupthink, peer pressure or personal biases. This is relevant, because the content we consume shapes how we react, how we show up and what we perceive to be attractive.

Physical environment is also an important factor. When you move from one place to another — for example, say you move from London to New York, or from a small town like my wife Jill's in Virginia to a big city — it's useful to have a checklist in your mind. How does the sex ratio impact how people are acting? As a result of that, what biases do I have when I am interacting with them? What do people find attractive here that maybe they didn't find attractive back home in London? And how is mate value being assigned? And even though you don't want to turn yourself into someone you're not, perhaps there are things you can manage about yourself or how you're showing up that will allow you to better connect with people and increase your perceived mate value in that environment (I go into how to manage your mate value in more detail in Chapter 6). This knowledge can also help to protect you from a sense that you have to conform to the status quo and give up those beliefs that are important to you.

CHANGING RELATIONSHIP EXPECTATIONS OVER TIME

As we've already seen, the goal of dating has changed dramatically over the years. If you go back a thousand years, arranged marriages were the norm throughout most of the world. Once the church intervened and people began to move from one place to another, that's when we started to see the rise of courtship. That courtship took on various forms at the outset, but mostly it was the man's responsibility, often with permission from his parents or some other external authority, to woo the parents of the woman — for example, with a dowry. And this didn't really change all that much until the 1960s and 1970s when women began to get independence that allowed them to have more say in which partner they chose. Just think about that: from the inception of marriage until the 'emancipation' of women, across almost every culture and socioeconomic level, the decision about who your partner was going to be was likely made by an external group, whether that was your clan, family, village, church, and so on. Now we mostly make this decision alone, which is a major change. Once this shift happened, that's really where all of the gameplay and strategy around dating — by all genders — began.

When you have your family or someone else making the choice on your behalf, they can make rational decisions. But the moment you have to make the decision mostly on your own, and you're in lust with the person, you begin to make irrational decisions.

Since women gained this greater independence, courtships have become longer and more casual over time. When my parents got married, they dated for a short period of time, and it was very structured. The end goal was marriage and 2.4 kids. Today it's, 'Let's have sex and hang out for a couple months and see where this thing takes us.'

The *Monitoring the Future* survey has been given to high-school seniors in the USA every year since 1975.[13] Two of the questions are 'Do you plan to be married?' and 'Do you plan to have children?' The percentage of people who plan to be married and have children has basically remained the same since 1975 — until we got to Gen Z, which was the first generation to have a majority of respondents say, 'I have no idea.'[14] And the data that I see with Tinder is that marriage is less and less what people are looking for.

Despite this, it is my belief that Gen Zers will have the strongest marriages of any generation. They'll also have the fewest marriages of any generation, but I predict they're going to have the lowest divorce rates and the strongest relationships because they're so focused on self-development, emotional vulnerability, strong communication and healing trauma. They believe in therapy and want someone who's unique. They prioritise kindness, and they're more inclusive. One of the best ways to combat sex ratios is to widen your pool, and now you have a generation that says, 'You know what, it doesn't matter where you come from or what race you are. Let's hang out and see where this goes.' Dating has evolved to a place where Gen Zers don't even like to call it dating — they're just hanging out.

A lot of traditionalists will look at that and say, 'That's not the way it should be done.' But you could argue that it's a more prudent way of going about things. They're rejecting exclusivity and just hanging out with different people to get to know and see the real them. And it's from there that they move on to commitment, which is still what 70 per cent say they want. It's a stark contrast to my grandmother in her village in Jamaica, who had very few men to choose from and was more or less pushed into marriage when she was eighteen. But it's what always happens. As society's needs and values change over time, so too do marriages and relationships more generally, a point made by Alex Gendler in his TED-Ed lesson 'The History of Marriage'.[15]

THE PROS AND CONS OF ONLINE DATING

Another big difference in the dating environment is the way that we meet people today. Online is now the number-one mechanism by which we find a significant other, regardless of sexual orientation — so much so that it's built into the culture. When I was growing up, the milestones were getting your driver's licence at sixteen and having your first (legal) drink at twenty-one. Today, people turn eighteen and download a dating app. There's good and bad with this. The bad is that it's made us ultra-conscious of the visual — a large part of the decision to connect with someone is based on their photo. It's true that in the past the decision about whether you would dance with someone at the school disco was probably largely influenced by how that person looked, but there's more depth to that assessment in real life.

Something else you see quite a lot with online dating is hypergamy. This seems particularly popular with highly educated women who are looking for long-term, committed partnerships. If a woman has a master's degree, for example, something like nine out of the ten people who she opts to connect with also have a master's degree or higher form of education. This comes down again to a perception of your own mate value. But dating apps have arguably reduced the fullness of mate value, because our decisions are based on relatively superficial qualities such as looks, education, title and profession. Whereas when you get a chance to interact with someone in real life, you understand that mate value has many other characteristics, such as confidence and charisma.

Another negative thing that online has done is give us a perception that there's an endless number of people out there for us to choose from, so we put less effort into our interactions. If you connect with ten people in the next hour on your app, it's a lot different than my grandmother who only had eight eligible men in her village. And with less at stake from each interaction, we have become lazier in terms of showcasing who we are and what we do.

But there are lots of positives to online dating. Apps allow us to meet people who we would not ordinarily interact with — for example, you can pinpoint the increase in interracial dating with the launch of Tinder. There's also a feedback loop built into online dating that most of us don't get in real life. If you put up your profile and you get no interactions, you know that you probably have to change something. This is very important for straight men, as they don't typically have a source of feedback in their day-to-day lives. A woman or gay man, on the other hand, may be more likely to go on a date and then tell their friends all about it. And those friends will give advice and support − 'maybe you should do this' or 'perhaps you should wear that'. This feedback sharpens their ability to then go back out on the next date, but straight men are much less likely to receive this type of advice from their friends. The feedback from online dating fills this gap. And this is taken even further with the rise of AI. Not only do you get the implicit feedback of how many hits you get, AI is built into the software so that when you start to write a message, the tool will flag anything that is potentially crude or off-putting. And this is great because it's non-judgemental feedback.

But the biggest issue with online dating is that it has been mislabelled − it should be called 'online meeting'. You don't date someone in an app − it is a tool to meet people, especially people you wouldn't otherwise have crossed paths with. Seen from this perspective, I am optimistic about the benefits of technology when it comes to finding love. Used correctly, it is a very powerful tool.

♥

At the end of the day, the most important thing when it comes to finding a partner is awareness — of your past, of yourself and of your environment. Let's say, for example, that you haven't healed from a trauma: you are more likely to suffer from confirmation bias when it comes to the behaviour associated with it. Or perhaps you are unaware of a trauma and its impact on you, leading you to have an anxious attachment style. If you add in an unawareness of your environment, then it is much more likely that you are going to think that the world is against you and that you can't win. This can lead to you pointing the finger outwards. This is why it's so important to recognise that there are forces both inside and outside of your influence that have a real impact on your search for love. Many of us have a tendency to put the blame on ourselves when things go wrong, but it's prudent to understand that someone might not be into you for a million reasons that you have little or no control over. And just knowing that helps you to show up more confidently, and when you are more confident, you show up as your authentic self, which is so important.

The truth is there's a significant amount that you can change about your search for a partner if only you are aware of the forces at play. With this awareness, you can head out into the world of dating with much more confidence that you will navigate it successfully and find the path that takes you to the top of the mountain.

KEY TAKEAWAYS

1. Evolution and the world in which we live, both forces outside of our control, make up the environment in which we look for love.

2. Mate value, cognitive biases and sex ratio are all evolutionary factors to be aware of when searching for a partner.

3. Online dating (which would be better thought of as 'online meeting') is the primary way people now meet their significant others, which brings both benefits and downsides.

'DON'T GIVE UP. ALL IT TAKES IS JUST ONE SMALL MOVE TO CHANGE YOUR ENTIRE DIRECTION'

5

THE PROS AND CONS OF DIFFERENT WAYS TO MEET A PARTNER

It's time to put some of the work that we've done so far into practice and get into the nitty-gritty of how to meet someone.

In my experience as a matchmaker, there are two primary issues when it comes to selecting a partner. The first of these is the actual selection − in other words, choosing the right person. Three of my favourite researchers on this subject are Eli Finkel, Sue Johnson and Esther Perel. Finkel would say that we're placing too much weight on each partner. Traditionally, you'd just choose someone who was going to fulfil one or two of your needs, but now we want the whole package.[1] Johnson, on the other hand, would say that because of our past trauma, we end up picking people who reinforce our negative behaviour. Say you have an abusive father, so you believe that abuse translates into love: you are more likely to go out and pick a similarly abusive partner.[2] Perel, meanwhile, talks about how we have a tendency to trade off the things we need for novelty. This person is the shiny object − perhaps they have a really cool accent or come from a different background − and this novelty factor makes that person more attractive.[3]

So, a lot of the research that is done is about the selection process. Then, when you go online or watch a dating show on television, the focus is almost always on the choosing of a partner too. But there is a second aspect to this that is less often talked about. And it wasn't until I started matchmaking that I realised how prevalent this problem is − in fact, it should really come first. I call it the 'pipeline problem'. If you're not interacting with enough potential partners, you can never get to the part where you make the selection. I believe a big reason why we end up choosing bad partners is because we meet so few people and limit our choices. Or we end up just being chosen.

The key to me in terms of optimising your ability to have a strong, long-term partnership is thinking about both of these things. Yes, you want to work on the selection (which we'll look at in more detail in Chapter 7), but you also need to increase the pipeline of people you are interacting with. And I want to underscore interaction, because one of the challenges with online dating and social media is that we believe we have an endless pool of people to choose from. Tinder might have been downloaded more than 530 million times, but that does not mean you have millions of potential matches. You need to interact with people. Matchmaking, however, has led me to understand how few people are actually dating and therefore interacting with anyone.

The dating apps regularly do surveys to better understand their users, and while they don't usually release the results, my experience has shown me that people on average are only going on a few dates a year. You also have to factor in the reality that a small percentage of users are dating frequently and the rest seldom or not at all. The Pew Research Center tells us that more than half those people in the USA who have never been married have used a dating app, so if you look at the total pool, it's going to be only a few dates at best for most people.[4] This is especially true of men. On many dating apps, a lot of men see zero engagement with their profiles — one reason for this is because they don't fully invest in the process and don't complete their biographies and only include one photo if any at all. For these men, no one swipes right and no one connects with them.

In matchmaking, it was not uncommon for us to have clients who had not been on a date in many years. This was in part because the pipeline has narrowed over time as a result of societal and cultural shifts, and the conduits by which we meet people in real life have shrunk. In the past, we had our friends and family, the church, the workplace (particularly in the twentieth century after women gained more independence) and the various social settings that emerged with the creation of leisure time, such as dance halls in the UK and drive-in movie theatres in the USA. Today, fewer of us go to church, and the workplace is increasingly becoming a no-go zone for romantic relationships.

With the rise of the internet and the shift towards online communication, these traditional conduits began to be replaced by the emergence of online dating from the mid-1990s. Then, as we've seen, in the last decade or so, following the introduction of dating apps such as Tinder (which was released in 2012), online has become one of the predominant ways of meeting a potential partner.

My wife and I sold our matchmaking agency in 2016, since when the pipeline has narrowed even further. Following the pandemic, far more people work at home. We buy more goods online rather than going to shops and the supermarket. Many of us exercise at home. We now live a much more isolated life with far less in-person interaction. This is another reason why online dating's popularity continues to rise.

It's also important to say that going on a date is simply the first step. When you go on a date, most of the time you don't see that person again. So, if you're only meeting a few people in real life each year, and most of those are not suitable, you could go a long time without having a strong candidate to choose from. That's when it becomes easy to take the first thing that comes along. If you go five years without a date and then meet someone who is just OK, you might be tempted to settle.

But why is all of this important? Well, a number of studies have been carried out that provide empirical evidence that when you have a larger dating pool, you make better choices and end up in a stronger partnership. For example, one study found that people who live in areas with a larger pool of potential partners (i.e. a greater number of unmarried individuals in the same age range) are more likely to get married and stay married than those who live in areas with a smaller pool.[5] And another study found that people who have a larger dating pool tend to be more selective in their choice of partner and are more likely to find someone who is a good match for them in terms of shared values, interests and goals.[6]

Eli Finkel has also done research that shows the larger pool you have, the better choices you make.[7] But it's important to emphasise that we mean an actual pool here as opposed to a perceived pool — it's not the perception that you have a million people to choose from online that matters; it's the people you actually interact with directly.

WIDENING YOUR POOL IN REAL LIFE

So, how do you enlarge your pipeline of potential matches? Despite the shift towards online dating, there are still countless ways to meet people in real life, via things like social and family events, common hobbies and interests, school and continuing education, restaurants, bars and clubs, festivals, public spaces such as dog-walking parks, gyms and other fitness classes, charity and volunteering, sporting events, museums and art galleries, or going to hear a speaker give a talk. I once gave a talk in Atlanta on relationships and a contestant from *The Apprentice* was seated in the front row, and a guy who had come to listen to me sat next to her. They had never met, and now they are married. I emceed their wedding, because they said they would never have met if it hadn't been for that event. You can even meet someone on a dating show such as *Love Is Blind* or *Married at First Sight*.

Travel as a means of meeting potential partners is also really big right now, especially as more people are open to borderless dating, a term I coined in Tinder's *The Future of Dating 2023* report. You can go to another country and be sitting in a coffee shop and meet someone, and the fact that you are from another country doesn't decrease your opportunity to connect with them, it actually increases it (see more about this in Chapter 6).

There are also lots of online activities that don't count as dating but still provide opportunities to meet people, social media being one obvious example. That's why I need to reiterate that 'online dating' is a misnomer. It's really 'online meeting'. Once you see it from that perspective, it becomes a bit easier, as the bar is lower. In general, you should think of it as, 'Where can I go to meet people?'

So, you're going to lots of places and meeting a lot of people in real life, and you therefore have a pretty big pipeline of people you're interacting with. The question then is, do you go into those situations intentionally thinking, 'This is going to be somewhere I'm going to meet someone'? Or is it more about just meeting people and you might end up having a connection with someone? The answer is: the two are not mutually exclusive. I believe you can say to yourself, 'Hey, I would love to meet a partner, but I'm also going to this event because I really want to.' Getting enjoyment out of what you do is the first and most important thing. That's the cake, and the icing is the chance you might meet someone. But it's important to keep both in mind, because if you're not thinking that you could potentially meet someone, you might overlook someone or you might not read a signal that they're attempting to send to you.

Body-language experts would tell you that men have a horrible time interpreting flirting and truly understanding if a woman likes them. Some guys just think every woman in the world is into them, whereas others presume the opposite — neither are necessarily reading the signals right. Either way, it's difficult to read someone when you are in the same room as them. It's even more difficult online. Meeting someone in real life therefore gives you a bit of a head start.

When you meet someone in real life, you've already gotten past some of the stages that you would have had to have gone through if you were online. Not only does this give you the chance to see what they're really like in the flesh, it also means there is probably already a connection point. You have gone to see the same author speak or have joined the same club because you have a shared interest. Or perhaps you have met at university, so you have a similar level of education. Whatever it is, having this initial point of common interest makes it more likely that you share the values that will ultimately allow you to connect with a strong partner.

The downside of trying to meet people in real life is efficiency. We are all busy people. That's one of the reasons why Tinder was such a game-changer — it was a mobile-first app, and it allowed you to very quickly interact with a large number of people.

We also have to keep in mind that fear is the number-one reason why men say they can't find a partner. When you're in a real-life situation, fear of rejection is even higher. If you're not going to walk up and approach someone, it's just not going to happen for you. As we discussed in Chapter 2, the majority of men would welcome it if a woman were to approach them, but a lot of women say that men don't like it if they do: 'I approached three guys in the past, and they all rejected me — I'll never do it again.' Even if that was simply because they weren't attracted to you, it hurts to be rejected, and it's sometimes easier to think that being rebuffed is because men don't like woman approaching them.

An extension of this is shame, and the inability to rebound from it. If I'm online and I swipe right on someone and they immediately turn me down, I can just go on to the next person, and there is no sense of lingering shame that is carried forward. Whereas if you interact with someone in real life and they turn you down, it's now public. This makes it less likely that you will want to engage with anyone in the first place.

It's also hard work to keep finding new opportunities to meet people in real life. Your family and friends are pretty stable, and they've probably already introduced you to the people they think might be suitable. Perhaps you've been in the same job for a long time, or maybe you're not comfortable approaching strangers in a bar. This is where a concept I've been playing around with for more than ten years, and which I deeply believe in, comes in, influenced by Mark Granovetter's theory about the importance of strengthening weak ties.[8]

We all have a social circle, some bigger than others. However, anthropologist and evolutionary psychologist Robin Dunbar has suggested that the limit of social connections that each of us is capable of is approximately

150 people.[9] If you were to line them up and rank them from best friend to the person you know least well, Mark Granovetter's theory states that we typically go to the friends who are nearest to us for help. That's where we most often look for the opportunities. So, you ask your best friend to hook you up with somebody. And we don't just go to those nearest friends when we're looking for romantic partners – we also go to them for business opportunities or when we want tickets to the game. But we have already exploited all of those connections. They've already tried for us. It is with the 150th friend, the one you haven't talked to in a while, where the real opportunities lie. That's where new job offers come from. And that's where romantic interests can be found.

My weakest ties are certainly where most of the opportunities in my life have originated. It's where all my big projects have come from, and it's how I ended up in the UK. The weak ties offer us the best chances to find what we want, because those connections haven't been fully exploited yet. I really believe it is the secret sauce.

There are three steps to strengthening your weak ties. The first is that you need to constantly introduce new people into your social circle. But that doesn't mean you need to be meeting potential romantic partners. It just means you need to be introducing new people into your life in general. A lot of people will probably say, 'Well, how do you do that?' In my case, I'm a bit of an introvert, and I actually hate going to events, although, strangely, I don't mind if I'm the one speaking. Whenever I have a dinner to go to, I'm always looking for excuses to get out of it. Knowing this about myself has meant that I've had to come up with ways to overcome my introversion. For example, I have been hosting brunches for a few years now, to which I'll invite people I don't know very well. The last brunch I did was twenty guys who were all in the entertainment industry in the UK. Some of them were people I had never met but respected from afar. It was a way of pulling them into my social circle and strengthening my weak ties. It doesn't mean that they will all stay in my network, but some might. You can do this on a smaller scale by inviting a friend of a friend or a work acquaintance for a coffee or lunch.

The second thing, and this is very important, is you have to cultivate your relationships with your weak ties. As you get older, your social circle tends to get smaller. Unfortunately, my best friend passed away a few years ago, and he was the more sociable of the two of us, so I met a lot of people through him. Following his death, not only did I find that I was meeting fewer new people,

I also realised I didn't cultivate the relationships I already had. So now, every week, I pick three people I haven't talked to in forever — two years, five years, ten years — and I'll just drop them a WhatsApp voice message: 'Hey, just checking in. I saw on your Instagram page that you got promoted. Congratulations!' Or, 'How are you? Jill and I and the boys moved to London. If you're ever here, look us up. Let's have dinner.' Cultivating those weak ties leads to opportunity.

The third piece is you have to think strategically about how you can actually add value to your weak ties. Because that's really how relationships form. It's not about 'how much can I take from you?' It's 'how much can I give?' If you haven't deposited enough in the giving account, you can't then make a withdrawal. I'm thinking all the time how I can help people. In fact, I just did this with a friend in the States. I saw that she'd done a segment on local TV in Atlanta, so I reached out to her and said, 'I know somebody who works at *Good Morning America*. Do you want me to send your segment to them? I can't promise that they'll put you on, but let me send it to them.' Her response was, 'Oh, Paul, I'd love that. Oh my gosh, that's incredible.'

I wasn't thinking about what I wanted to take from this person further down the line — it would be fine if she never did me a favour in the future. My thinking was, 'She is a weak tie of mine, and I want to cultivate my weak ties, so I'm just going to give, and you never know what might come of it.' I truly believe that doing this sort of thing has been the best thing I've done for my career.

This strategy translates to romantic opportunities too. In addition to everything else that we've talked about, strengthening your weak ties helps you to widen your pipeline, and to ensure that those coming through it are of high quality. Adding a new person to your social circle means that the connection holding the 150th position drops out. But it's OK to fire friends and say goodbye to people when you are no longer adding value to each other's lives. Then, if the new person stays in your circle, it typically means that they have shared values and interests with you and your current group of friends. This in turn means that their social circle of 150 friends probably overlaps a lot with your and your friends' values and interests. Think about that. Just as Mark Granovetter described, that person becomes the bridge to a whole new circle of people you've probably never met before, some of whom are going to be single. By strengthening your weak ties and introducing a new person into your life, you've also widened the pipeline of potential partners, many of whom are likely to share your values and interests — that's what I mean by high quality.

MEETING PEOPLE ONLINE

While there are many ways of meeting people in real life, and this might be preferable for a lot of people, the reality is online is such a big part of dating today that it can't be ignored. If you want to maximise the size of your pool of potential partners, you have to take advantage of every means at your disposal.

Although online dating came to prominence in the twenty-first century, most people probably don't realise that it really started in the 1960s. And it began where a lot of tech ideas come from: a prestigious university. In 1965, three Harvard undergraduates by the names of Jeffrey C. Tarr, David L. Crump and Vaughan Morrill created Operation Match for students of Ivy League universities. Users filled out a questionnaire and returned it with a fee. Their answers were then run through a computer algorithm and, a couple of weeks later, a list of matches and their telephone numbers was sent back. It was all about matching people based on their interests and values. One of the things I find most interesting about Operation Match is that it didn't include a photo, and there were very few questions about attractiveness — the only one was along the lines of 'How important is attractiveness to you?' When you fast-forward to today, it's all about photos.

Although Tarr and Crump later set up a business called Compatibility Research, Inc. with a former Cornell student called Douglas H. Ginsburg, who went on to become a senior judge, computer dating didn't really take off for another thirty years with the introduction of Match.com in 1995. This was an online dating site that again centred around a long list of questions, although there was now the option to upload photos too. This was followed by other popular sites, such as eHarmony, which had an almost 14 per cent share of the US dating-services market in 2015.[10] This was the year that the online dating landscape changed for ever with the intro-duction of Tinder, the first mobile dating app. This allowed quick access and introduced the concept of the swipe feature in dating — swipe right if you're inter-ested, swipe left for no — simplifying the process compared with the previous generation of web-based dating sites (the eHarmony questionnaire had as many as 450 questions at one point).

Tinder also opened up the dating landscape to casual dating, or what we now know evolutionary psychologists would call short-term mating, leading to it being known as the hook-up app. The developers realised that a lot of people don't start out wanting a long-term partner and that the dating landscape is made up of people with all sorts of different relationship goals. Tinder was the first to say, 'There is no judgement — everybody is welcome to jump into this party.' As a result, it became the cool spot. As well as convenience, people want to be at the place where everybody else is. When I was at college, some of my friends always wanted to go to the club that was known to have the most women. They didn't care where it was or what music it was playing as long as it was where the majority of women were likely to be. A big part of the success of Tinder was the sense that every-body was there, and it quickly became the number-one dating app, and it's continued to retain the top spot in the world today.[11]

Tinder and the other apps that followed it soon pro-ceeded to double down on the features that really worked, like photos. And as online dating has developed further over the years, it's changed how we go about seeking a partner and what we're looking for in a rela-tionship. For example, Tinder doesn't ask its users to designate things like ethnicity or education. It's what we call frictionless dating, based around the belief that it's to your advantage to meet people outside of your social circle. It's back to those weak ties, right? You want to introduce new people into your social circle, because when you do, you're not just introducing that person, you're introducing their network too. So Tinder's position was that they wanted to open it up to everyone.

When other dating apps entered the market, these newcomers figured they couldn't compete with the shopping mall, so they instead decided to build boutique stores. There was the app for all the farmers. The app for the left-handers. Then the app for the left-handed farmers. The apps became increasingly niche to the point that a big player like Hinge realised that some people like to search based on type and allowed you to opt in to a silo for education, a silo for ethnicity, a silo for age, and so on.

However, I believe that we're now reaching a point where interrelationships — interracial, interreligious, international — will be the standard and not the exception. On Tinder, 61 per cent of users have dated someone of a different ethnicity and 80 per cent are open to marrying someone of a different ethnicity, while 70 per cent are open to someone of a different religion.[12] And you have people identifying in a more diverse way than they ever have before. So, long story short, I think frictionless dating and not pushing people into silos is the future, because that's what Gen Z wants, and, as we've seen, it makes up the majority of the dating population.

One of the major benefits of online dating is that it's actually quite empowering. You're more in control, and you're able to make connections in a way that feels safe. There's not the same fear or sense of shame. And you can meet people who have the same relationship goals as you and assess if there's some level of compatibility right off the bat.

Your potential matches can also be from anywhere in the world. Tinder has a feature called Passport, which allows you to select a city in another country and look for people there. On Tinder Passport, London is the number-one city in the world. I have an American friend, a popular television personality, who thinks she's going to meet her husband in London. In fact, I suspect a lot of Americans think they're going to meet their prince or princess there.

The downside to this is that, if you can select someone from any city in the world, it can be pretty overwhelming. It also means that you can be rejected by anyone in the world. And it's painful to be rejected. The sting of rejection is relative. For some people, being rejected online could have as much of an impact as someone else being publicly humiliated. As a result of all of this, people can become disgruntled with online dating very quickly.

Men in the incel movement — 'incel' being short for 'involuntary celibate' — are at the extreme end of this spectrum, as they are not even willing to engage in the process. Because they believe it's a zero-sum game and that they're not going to win, they choose to opt out and instead place the blame on women. This extreme reaction speaks to the disillusionment that can arise with dating. It can be a difficult and tiring process, especially if you have to meet a lot of people in order to maximise your chances of finding someone suitable. With online dating, a lot of people drop out after three months — some because they have found a match but many out of frustration. Often, though, these people come back, and a cycle of leaving and then returning develops.

Another downside of online dating is that there's a significant amount of fraud, ranging from catfishing to financial. In fact, financial romance fraud, whereby someone is tricked into entering a relationship so that money can be stolen from them, is one of the fastest growing types of fraud in the United States at the time of writing.[13] This is why online safety has become an increasing focus for apps such as Tinder, leading to them building in features that deter fraud, as well as preventing crude messages and any photos apart from those on your profile from being shared.

Then there is the time needed to maintain your profile and keep on top of your potential matches and messages. People work long hours, and they often use work devices which aren't suitable for personal use. So even though apps have in some ways made the process of meeting people easier, some users still feel like they don't have a lot of time to devote to it and accessibility can still be a challenge.

The next disadvantage of online dating is perhaps going to sound a bit strange, but a lot of men report that they don't feel like they have good photos of themselves to upload. When I joined Tinder as their Global Research Expert, I remember talking to people in the company about how horrendous the men's photos were. They were holding a fish they'd caught. Or they didn't have a shirt on and were leaning up against a car. Just terrible photos. But I wasn't in a great place to criticise. So that I could better understand the app and how it was used, I set up an account. It took me a while to find a good photo, and I was in the matchmaking business! I then had a call with the Head of Product Development, and she told me my photo was terrible too — and she was right. I didn't have any good photos of myself. It's a big issue for a lot of guys, because photos have become central to the online dating experience.

This shift in emphasis from no photos in the early days to photos being so important has benefits and downsides. On the plus side, an image tells a thousand words, and you could argue that a photo allows for a better sense of a person than text alone. However, this only holds true if the photos are authentic. When photos first came into vogue on dating sites in the late 1990s, a lot of people would use a professional headshot. The common response to that was, 'Well, that's not really how you look on a day-to-day basis.' It was also expensive to get a professional image, so you'd only get one or two, and you'd have that professional image for years. Even people who didn't get a professional photo taken would instead use old photos of themselves. It got to the point that the average age of a photo was ten years old. No one looks like they did ten years ago. We all like to think we do, but unfortunately we don't.

Over the years, this issue of authenticity has only been exacerbated by the introduction of filters and photo editing. People naturally want to know if what they are seeing is really you or your digitally enhanced representative. And this is important, because being physically attracted to someone is still very important. It's not just about connecting on an intellectual or emotional level. You still have to like the look of someone.

The bottom line is that a dating site or app is a tool, and it can be used badly or it can be used well. So even before worrying about how good your photos are, make sure you include some in the first place. You would think this is obvious, but a lot of people don't include any photos at all, even though a high percentage of the decision to engage with you is based on what you look like. And having multiple photos is better, because the data shows that if you have three to five photos, you will be engaged with more than if you have just one. And why is that? Because of the authenticity problem — if people only see one photo, they're not sure it's actually you. This issue is also being helped by apps like Tinder introducing photo verification.

So, you need to have the right number of photos, but you also need to have the right types of photos. There are three kinds that are optimal. Number one is a photo of you smiling a nice, authentic smile. So how do you do that? Ask somebody to tell you a joke and have them fire off a couple of photos at the same time. Number two is a full-body shot, because the truth is everyone wants to see what your body looks like. And I think we put a little bit more pressure on that than we need to. Instagram has obviously reshaped what we think is a standard level of physical attractiveness, but in essence people are again just looking to see that it's really you, and also that you conform broadly to the golden mean I mentioned previously (see page 95). And even if you don't, different people are attracted to and prioritise different things. Also, Tinder's *The Future of Dating 2023* revealed that many people are now saying that feeling comfortable with someone is of higher importance than physical attractiveness.[14] The third photo is one of you doing an activity that you're passionate about. This is much more engaging than just a photo of you on a night out drinking.

Next, you need to complete your profile. And I mean really complete it, because online dating is a computer system, and the algorithms will favour you if you have filled out all of the questions and uploaded your photos. This is because the app wants to showcase people who look like they're fully using and engaging with it. Then, when it comes to the content of your profile, you should stay away from saying all the things you don't want. Talk about what you are interested in as opposed to what you are not interested in. This is a much better way of getting across your values. These tips might all seem very basic, but they are the keys to optimising your profile, and you'd be surprised, in my experience, how many people don't do it.

Of course, creating your profile is only half the battle. To use a dating app or site effectively, you actually have to engage with people. Someone's profile can only tell you so much, and your goal is probably not to establish a relationship online – you therefore need to meet potential matches in real life. People are typically very meticulous, and it's not uncommon for someone to spend thirty or forty minutes on a dating app and not engage with anyone in that time, but this is not the approach I'd recommend – you really need to engage with as many people as possible. This means being open to people who you are even remotely interested in and getting to the point where you're actually meeting them in real life so you can really make your assessment.

Whether you meet someone in real life or online, authenticity is the name of the game. Baby boomers, Gen Xers and millennials are much quicker to lie in their profiles. But Gen Z is really all about authenticity and what I call embracing the quirk – in my opinion, it's a much healthier way of going about things. The key is to stand out based on your individuality. You want to be utterly true to yourself, and you want to be so transparent in terms of who you are and what you believe that it might even push some people away. This is why we're beginning to see more people include political and social beliefs in their dating profiles.

I realise that not everyone is good at talking about themselves or putting themselves forward and identifying what their virtues are, but you can get help from other people. Ask your friends and family to look at your profile and photos so that they can give you honest feedback. You can even hire a dating coach. And AI is being heavily integrated into dating apps right now, which can help you to create a narrative around your likes and interests. So you can definitely get assistance on this. But whether you do it yourself or you get some help, try to use online dating well; otherwise, you're probably better off not using it all.

STAYING OPEN-MINDED

Throughout the process of meeting new people, it's so important to remain open-minded. When I worked as a matchmaker, most of my clients were hard-charging professionals in their forties. When they hired me, right out of the gate they would give me a long list of things they wanted in a partner. I had one client who gave me a spreadsheet of about 150 things she wanted in a husband — no exaggeration — even down to him having good feet, along with photos to illustrate what she meant. This was an extreme example, but the majority of people I worked with were highly engaged and, in my opinion, fairly close-minded.

Meanwhile, my oldest client was in her late seventies. And to be honest, I was reluctant to take her on, but I did, because I liked a challenge. When I sat down to do my intake call with her, I was ready for her to give me a long list of requirements. Instead, she said, 'Paul, I'm in my seventies. Do you know how hard it is to find a man my age who can walk up the stairs to my apartment? I want you to find me a man who can walk up three flights of stairs.'

I said, 'OK, what else?'

'That's it.'

'Are you serious?'

'Yes, I'm absolutely serious. I only want you to find me a man who can walk up three flights of stairs to my apartment.'

Once I got over my surprise, I realised that she was very wise. As well as being an indicator of good general health, she was also telling me that she was completely open-minded. She was saying, 'I don't care about ethnicity. I don't care about religion. I don't care if they have five children or no children. I'm just looking for a companion for the rest of my life.' Having only one requirement is at the opposite end of the spectrum to my client with the spreadsheet, and I realise that's not realistic for most of us, but the closer we are to that point, the richer the pool becomes.

It all comes back to the size of your pipeline. If you only have one requirement, your pipeline of potential matches is going to be much wider than someone with 150 items on their wish list. And you want your pipeline to be as wide as possible so more fish can swim through it, and then you can whittle down the numbers through your interactions. Most people start with a super narrow pipeline — you need to have good feet just to get in — and when you do that, you severely limit your potential matches. In fact, you can soon start to believe that this person doesn't exist. And that is a very dangerous place to be.

♥

If the most important thing is to widen your pool, the best strategy is to use every tool at your disposal. So it's not just about going down the online route or trying to meet people in real life — it's about meeting as many people as you can, however you can. Yes, a lot of people now meet their significant other online, but that leaves a large number of people who are meeting at work, or in bars, or at the gym, or in a myriad of other settings. Use it all. And use it optimally. Whether you're online or meeting in real life, show up as your best self — engage.

Jeff Bezos is widely quoted as saying, 'Your brand is what other people say about you when you're not in the room.'[15] In other words, it's not what you say it is; it's how you're perceived by others. In dating, you could call it your mate value rather than your brand, but the principle holds true: you need to make a good impression on other people. So regardless of whether you are intentionally looking for a new partner or just trying to meet new people, come as your best self and good things will happen.

KEY TAKEAWAYS

1. One of the main issues people face when looking for a partner is not meeting enough people.

2. You can increase your pool of potential partners by maximising the number of people you meet in real life and by using online dating effectively.

3. One of the best strategies you can employ to meet new people is strengthening your weak ties.

'NO ONE HAS LIVED THE LIFE THAT YOU'VE LIVED. NO ONE HAS ENGAGED WITH THE PEOPLE YOU'VE ENGAGED WITH. NO ONE WHO HAS EVER WALKED THIS PLANET HAS HAD THE SAME EXPERIENCES AS YOU. YOU'RE UNIQUE BEYOND BELIEF. YOU ARE EXTRAORDINARY'

6

MAXIMISING YOUR CHANCES OF FINDING A PARTNER

Before we move on to the criteria that you should be looking for in a partner in the next chapter, there is another equally important piece of the selection puzzle that we need to focus on, and that is improving your chances of meeting someone suitable and making yourself as appealing as possible.

When it comes to the most important things in life, most people don't say, 'Oh, I'm just going to let my career unfold as it will.' Or, 'I'm just going to fall into a good university.' Or, 'I'm going to become healthier just by manifesting it.' Most of us are intentional about these aspects of our lives. Finding our romantic partners should be no different.

To be intentional, you need goals. Some people might say that not having any goals means you can't be disappointed, but I think the opposite is true. I feel like when you don't have a goal, you set yourself up for disappointment, because the research shows that people in relationships without goals have lower levels of satisfaction.[1] And goals in general help us to get the most out of life.

When a lot of us say that we don't have relationship goals, the truth is we do have them — we just don't want to verbalise what they are. There are so many factors as to why that might be the case. Perhaps it has something to do with a person's culture. Or maybe it is a symptom of some sort of trauma from their past. Or it can be about their age. Gen Z, for example, refuses to label anything when it comes to relationships. As I mentioned before, Gen Zers don't even want to call dating 'dating', because they feel like the term doesn't speak to what they're doing. One of the reasons for this is that they want to be thought of as unconventional and unique. But it's also about self-value and self-worth — they don't want to scare someone off by professing what it is that they desire, because the other person might not desire the same thing, so there's also potentially a fear factor at play here.

But if you don't say what you want, you can't put a plan in place, and you end up being selected, as opposed to choosing and making the selection. So this chapter is really about using your goals and utilising the best strategies to find the partner that you want.

As we've seen, we haven't really bridged the gap of thinking there's nothing empirical about falling in love versus using all of this new data we have from relationship studies. Romanticism is often at the heart of this. Many of us still believe that love is in the air and it just happens, and this creates a cloud of confusion, because we need intentionality, and we need to be strategic.

This is even more the case when you consider that it is in many ways harder to find a partner today, because it's difficult to find the one person who's going to help you on the path towards self-actualisation. That's a much higher bar than finding someone who is going to protect you from lions and bears. Millions of people can keep you safe from physical danger, but very few are going to be able to help you to be your best self.

This means the weight of the decision of who you choose is greater than it's ever been. That being the case, what allows you a higher likelihood of reaching that goal is to have some sort of strategy — a goal and a plan. As I said earlier, I can't think of any aspect of our lives that we leave purely to luck. Even people who play the lottery have strategies. And studies show that strategies deliver results.[2]

The first thing you need to do is identify your over-arching relationship goal (see chapters 1 and 3) and be clear that you're going after a committed, long-term partnership, for example. The beauty of setting a goal like this is it then tells you all the things that you're not interested in — knowing that you want a long-term rela-tionship means that you can say no to the multitude of other types of relationships out there. This also allows you to structure your boundaries. In my opinion, bound-aries are just standards, and the higher standards we have, the higher quality of life we typically have, right across the board.

THE PREMIUM EFFECT

The next thing to consider is the premium effect, a con-cept I formed when my wife and I had our matchmaking agency in Washington, DC, which is a very metropolitan city. Often we would have two clients who were pretty much the same type of person — they were roughly the same age, worked for the government and made more or less the same amount of money — but one person would end up having loads of dates and the other would have almost none and be super annoyed. When we looked closer, the only difference we could find was that one of them was not born in Washington, DC and had just moved to the area. And because they'd just arrived, everything was new, everything was fresh and everything was exciting to them. As a consequence, their mate value (see page 162) was higher in the marketplace, and there would be more interest in them. If you were to take two people who had roughly the same profiles but one was from outside of the DMV (DC, Maryland and Virginia), there would be a better response to the person who wasn't from the area.

Our business focused on Black women at first, because they were being underserved in the matchmaking space. And, recognising that the premium effect meant there was a benefit to standing out, one of the things we would do was place a profile for our clients on, say, a Jewish dating app. Putting Black Christian women on a Jewish dating app might sound strange, but their inboxes were inundated with men who were interested in meeting them. Once we'd screened out the people who were fetishising what they perceived to be exoticism, and the people who were ignorant had screened themselves out by being inappropriate and revealing their prejudice, we were left with a good number of people who were attracted to our clients just because they were curious. They liked coming across someone who was different and new in their environment, and they wanted to ask questions, beginning with, 'Why are you on this app?' So, by putting our clients in these situations, we were actively weeding out the ignorant people, who make the worst partners anyway, and finding people who were open-minded and curious. And this was important, because those who are curious have among the highest marital satisfaction rates.[3]

We started to play around with this concept, placing our clients in environments, digitally or in real life, where they were the only one, and the results were exceptional. And I then started to use the premium effect in my professional life. That's one of the reasons why I took a job in the UK — as an American on television here, I thought I'd stand out. My first series after I moved was *Celebs Go Dating*. When it aired, I'll never forget, there was a bunch of ignorant comments: 'Who is this Yankee?', 'What does he know?', 'He doesn't know our culture.' There will always be an ignorant minority, but most people responded to me well.

And the open-minded, curious majority is growing. This is what the Tinder research is showing us as well, especially with Gen Z, which, as we have seen, is much more open to difference when it comes to dating, whether that be race, religion or geography.[4] When I started matchmaking, I remember clients rejecting good matches because they lived outside of the state, even if the state line was only an hour away. Today, some of us are open to dating people from around the world.

Awareness that people are becoming more open to differences can empower you, because your uniqueness becomes your superpower. No one has lived the life that you've lived. No one has engaged with the people you've engaged with. No one who has ever walked this planet has had the same experiences as you. You're unique beyond belief. You are extraordinary. Owning this is very important, as it is what gives you the confidence to step into situations and places where you are different from everyone else. A hypothetical example of this might be a white woman from Hertfordshire who attended an event at the Black Cultural Archives in Brixton in London. She would stand out, and other curious people there would gravitate towards her.

THE POWER OF AN INTRODUCTION

The next step is to be aware of how you are introduced to people. This is very important because introductions still remain one of the main ways of meeting someone who might become a long-term partner and then staying in a relationship with that person.[5] After all, even royals can meet that way. Meghan Markle and Prince Harry were introduced on Instagram. Harry was looking at a friend's account and saw a photo of her with Meghan. He then reached out to the friend and asked for an introduction.

But why are introductions so important? Robert Cialdini says that the level at which we are introduced to someone has a significant impact on the relationship we can form with them.[6] Let's say that you are at a business event, and you are introduced to someone by your mutual boss, as opposed to being introduced by another colleague at the same level as you. If you respect this boss — it can't be a boss whom you hate — this introduction will function like an endorsement. That person enters your social circle at a higher level of respect — not the same level as your boss, but relatively close.

When Oprah Winfrey, who is loved and revered by millions of people, introduced me to the American public as a matchmaker on her show, she could have said anything and that would have defined what I was for those people. Thankfully, she said I was much more than just a matchmaker. And, from that moment, that's what I was to everyone who holds her in high regard. Almost immediately, I received offers left, right and centre, and our matchmaking agency was inundated with clients. That's the power of a good introduction.

Knowing this means that it's important to harness this power effectively by soliciting introductions from people you respect and who are likely respected by others. In other words, it's a good strategy to seek introductions from people who have the highest level of respect in other people's social circles. This is particularly important if you're going into a situation where you're trying to meet new people and you have your defences up due to past trauma or previous failed relationships. Or perhaps you don't feel totally confident in your approach. If you get an endorsement via a strong introduction, it's a really great way of breaking down the barriers you might have erected. This is also the reason why you need to strengthen and activate weak ties who can make strong introductions on your behalf (as we explored in the previous chapter).

And the beauty is that everyone in your network is 'senior' to someone. For example, you might have a friend who is junior in their position at work, but they are a respected yoga instructor. Getting an introduction from them to someone in their yoga class would be a strong endorsement.

In his work on persuasion, Robert Cialdini identified seven key principles that contribute to someone being influential: reciprocity, commitment and consistency, social proof, authority, liking, scarcity, and unity.[7] Of these, I think 'liking' and 'reciprocity' have the most relevance to dating.

The concept of 'liking' is closely connected to something called the propinquity effect. This says that the closer you are to someone physically and psychologically, and the more familiar you are with them, the higher the chance you will like them. If you are stranded on a desert island with someone you despise, there is good chance that by day 365 you'll be firm friends. The closer in proximity you are to someone, the more likely it is that you will attach and bond with them. Cialdini says something similar: when you demonstrate that you like someone, there's a higher likelihood that they're going to like you back. It's kind of that simple.

I mentioned earlier that some guys have a perception that women like them more than they actually do. Well, that's also the reason why those same guys have no problem talking to women — they believe those women already like them. If they knew those women wanted nothing to do with them, they would most likely not engage or interact with them.

The concept of 'liking' also speaks to the notion that the more likeable you are, the more attractive you're going to be. And part of that is just being around someone, sharing interests and getting to know them.

'Reciprocity' is even more straightforward — it's 'I do for you, and you do for me'. It also relates to the idea of propinquity, because it is about building a relationship over time. You can't just sit at opposite ends of the beach on that desert island if you want to bond. You need to communicate and help one another out. Being reciprocal will help you to attach and have a deeper emotional connection.

DON'T BE QUICK TO JUDGE

How you approach a potential partner is also so important. It's vital to seem engaged and enthusiastic, and to demonstrate that you like someone to make yourself attractive to them in the first instance. This is where having an open mindset comes in again. As I've said before, most of my matchmaking clients were forty-something, hard-charging, upper-management, no-nonsense-type people. A lot of them were also single mums, so they had to get things done. When they went on dates, we'd sometimes be in the same place to observe them. Often, they'd sit across from their dates and, right away, from their body language, you could see they were creating a list in their minds of all the things that they despised about the person before them.

Afterwards, we'd do a debrief, and they'd say things like, 'He chewed with his mouth open', 'I could smell his breath from here', 'You should have seen the way he was holding his fork.' Our response would be to ask them to reframe the question: 'Yes, you have a list of several things you despised about your date, but let's throw that away. Let's weed in as opposed to weeding out and look for green flags as opposed to red. I know there were lots of things you didn't like, but give me two things that you did like.' Having an open mindset means being open to the possibility that there's a point of commonality that can be built on.

A closed mindset is walking into a date and saying that the person is not attractive enough for you. But that's just one characteristic, and the person you are discounting could be the kindest, humblest, least neurotic person in the world. An open mindset, on the other hand, is saying that your date is not the most attractive person you've ever seen, but there's something there. It's seeing the possibility and understanding that your attraction can grow over time. I've never seen any data to suggest that physical attraction can grow if there is zero there to begin with, but I've personally seen from my matchmaking work that if there is a minimal level of physical attraction at the outset, then it absolutely can increase over time, especially as the propinquity effect takes hold.

Having this mindset is so important because these more surface-level qualities, like attractiveness, are not the ones that are going to sustain a relationship in the long term. And you therefore have to be open-minded to get beyond those if they're not quite what you hoped for in the first instance.

You've probably heard endless tips about what you should be looking for on a first date. Were they on time? How did they treat the server? Did they hold the door open for you? But none of that really means anything. Why? Because none of the pieces that matter for a sustained relationship can be determined in that way. Instead, you just need to look for two things on a first date: do you have a minimal level of physical attraction to the person, and did they listen to you? That is the starting point for that mysterious thing we call chemistry.

Someone who listens to you and to whom you are at least a little bit physically attracted, and they are physically attracted to you and you listen to them, is what allows you to say, 'Let's start this journey.' Because that's what it is — a journey of getting to know one another and exploring the actual behaviours and characteristics that will determine if you can have a strong relationship. The fact that someone showed up ten minutes late could mean lots of things about that person's character. But guess what? It could just mean that they were running late from work. It doesn't mean that they are an asshole. You cannot determine what someone's really like up front.

It's also worth being aware that you're not necessarily going to meet the right person on the first date — you have to be willing to meet lots of people and go through this process with faith that you will meet someone eventually. Faith is such a huge piece of the puzzle. Sadly, a lot of people believe that love is not possible for them.

When I was matchmaking, I would say that my primary job was to give people hope. Whenever I had a new client, I knew that statistically they would probably not meet their spouse through me. But I could stop them from becoming demoralised and help them to create hope. A key way of doing this was showing them that there was a strategy that they could use and, by using that strategy and not leaving things to chance, the likelihood of them finding a partner shot through the roof. And going through the process was actually helping them to increase their social capital, which benefited them in all aspects of their lives. For example, dating skills like good conversation and confidence, along with knowing what you need and what your value is, are all things that will help you to be successful outside of romantic relationships.

It's also about having resilience in order to be able to keep going when things get tough. And that's one of the characteristics you need in a partner as well — they have to be resilient (more of which in the next chapter).

SOCIAL CAPITAL

The question I've received most often since entering the matchmaking space is, 'Paul, how do I find love?' And over the years, I've come up with a number of different answers. But now that I'm something of a veteran in this field, I can look back and say that the number-one way to find love, in my opinion, is to increase your social capital. I passionately believe that.

To me, social capital is made up of all the assets that we acquire in life. So, it is the network you've built. It's the experiences you've had, good and bad, and the lessons you've drawn from those experiences. It's how you express yourself. It's the skills that you have — perhaps you can paint or play the piano. It's your passions and hobbies. All of these things are assets that make up the treasure trove of who we are. And the more that we increase that capital, the higher mate value we have.

In the past, there was more benefit to being part of the pack, but we now live in a day and age in which individuality is highly valued. This not only separates us from the pack, it also elevates our mate value. This is perhaps the reason why so many of us gravitate towards people who are exceptional. I wrote a column and hosted a digital show for the newspaper *USA TODAY* that was called 'Uncommon Drive', for which I interviewed people whom I considered to be world-class in their chosen fields. I spoke to musicians, billionaire businesspeople, athletes — it didn't matter what they did as long they were among the most exceptional people in their area of expertise.

The reason I got that job was because I worked for Oprah Winfrey, who's considered to be exceptional in lots of areas, and, before that, I worked for Enver Yücel, the billionaire in Istanbul whom I mentioned in the Introduction — he runs one of the largest educational holdings in the world. I noticed that, on paper, they were completely different, yet they exhibited some of the same behaviours, and it was these behaviours that had helped them to become billionaires. So I wrote an article called 'Ten Things I Learned from Two Billionaires', and it went viral, and that's ultimately how I got the job at *USA TODAY*.

I say all of this to underscore my obsession with studying people who are exceptional. And what I saw was that those folks who were exceptional had this incredible level of social capital, and this is what had given them the opportunity to succeed. For example, one part of social capital is your network. So going back to Mark Granovetter, the more social capital you have, the stronger your network is. Maybe people in your network introduce you to new business partners. Or maybe they introduce you to a potential love match.

I'm passionate about relationship science, and that forms part of my social capital. The more I perfect my skills, if you will, within the realm of relationship science, the more that lifts up everything else. The better I am at what I do, the more my network wants to work for me. There's this symbiotic relationship between all of the assets that make up my social capital. So, when I say you need to work on your social capital, what I mean is, identify the things in your life that you're passionate about and work towards becoming exceptional at them. And it's like a tide — it lifts up everything else, including your romantic life. You get the network, the connections, the introductions; you get the spotlight, you're in new places, you're happier and more satisfied. And that means your pool is wider, your mate value is higher and the people you are meeting are better candidates to become your long-term partner.

Now, I'm not suggesting you have to be the number-one person in your field or become a billionaire — it's not the destination that matters. As long as you're on the journey towards becoming your best self, that's what's really important. And the further you travel on that journey, the more you'll get out of life. It also signals to other people that you're in pursuit of the top of the pyramid of Maslow's hierarchy of needs (see page 12). It tells them that you are someone who is going to be trustworthy, and curious, and kind. You being on that journey tells them that you are likely to have the qualities that most people need in a partner (which I discuss in the next chapter).

This again speaks to the importance of standing out. It seems as though fewer people want to be exceptional these days, so anyone who is in pursuit of excellence stands out even more. Which is just as well when you consider the incredible amount of choice that's out there. I mentioned before that one of the biggest problems on Tinder is straight men not completing their profiles. But merely adding a second photo vastly increases the percentage of click-throughs you receive, and this is only one step beyond mediocrity, so just imagine how much you can stand out if you are aiming to be the best you can be.

I think one of the reasons that fewer people want to be exceptional is that we're less hopeful in general and more dismayed about some of the things that are happening in the world right now. There's also so much more information flow, about COVID, financial crises, the cost of living, and it just beats us down and beats us down and beats us down.

In his book *Of Boys and Men*, Richard Reeves discusses that men have fallen substantially behind in many life categories, education being the most obvious.[8] Part of the reason for this is sedation, with some young men at home habitually smoking marijuana and watching porn. So men are disproportionately even less hopeful about the future, which again helps to explain why exceptionalism is just not a thing right now.

But I'm adamant that the more hopeful you are, the more exceptional you are, the more you're going to shine. That's why there's still real value in pursuing your passions and standing out. On *Celebs Go Dating*, we stage parties that include members of the general public. The celebs come in and mingle with the 'civilians', who have all been cast, and then they figure out who they want to go on a date with. Every time, there's a member of the public who comes in with amazing energy. They're confident, they're happy to talk with people, they're optimistic. And I don't just mean with the celebs. Even when the camera is off, they're communicating with the producers and interacting with us experts. Almost all of the time, that person ends up in the next episode or series. Whether it's the celebrity who picks them, or the director, or me or my co-host, their energy and enthusiasm pays off.

Typically, when the lights are on, somebody's going to knock on your door. So always try to show up as your best self — that way you'll stand out from the crowd and increase your chances of finding the right person for you.

♥

To reiterate, it's better to look for positives than negatives, and try not to get hung up on small things like, for example, the way someone talks. Or this one, which I hear all the time and which really pains me: 'He was lovely, but you should have seen what he was wearing.' To a certain degree, I understand — what we wear can be an important signifier of personality for some people. But what those people are doing is taking something small and assigning meaning that might not be right. Someone not being well-dressed could just mean that person has a heap of work and didn't have time to pick out something better. Or it could mean that they haven't been on a date in a while and didn't know what to wear. But none of those things tells you if the person is someone who could be a good match for you in the long term.

You have to keep your eye on the bigger picture and the things that really matter. There's enough data out there now to tell us exactly what qualities we should really be looking for if we want a partner who's going to deliver us a high level of relationship satisfaction. I therefore want to empower you to give up the fifty things that mean nothing and instead focus on what is really important when looking for love. Those fifty things need to take a seat, because they've not helped you thus far, and they're not going to help you going forward. Instead, it's time to identify the things we really need if we want to find lasting love.

KEY TAKEAWAYS

1. Being intentional and using strategies can increase your chances of meeting the right person for you.

2. Utilising the premium effect, harnessing the power of strong introductions and taking advantage of the propinquity effect can help boost your search for love.

3. Increasing your social capital and standing out from the crowd by working towards becoming exceptional at something you are passionate about will make you more attractive to potential partners.

'CHOOSE SOMEONE WHO MATCHES YOUR VALUES. CHOOSE SOMEONE WHO WILL CHALLENGE YOU TO GROW. CHOOSE SOMEONE WHO HAS PROVEN TO REMAIN CONSISTENT IN CHARACTER DURING GOOD TIMES AND BAD TIMES'

7

GREEN FLAGS: THE FIVE FUNDAMENTALS YOU SHOULD BE LOOKING FOR IN A PARTNER

In the previous chapter, I discussed strategies to make yourself as appealing as possible to potential partners. In this one, I'm going to cover the positive qualities that you should be looking for in the person who you're out there trying to find. Let's refer to these as green flags.

Ultimately, what I'm talking about here is choosing a partner wisely. And this is so important because, as I've said before, we typically don't choose, we're chosen. Or if we do choose, we're using criteria that do not contribute to relationship satisfaction.

In episode 1 of season 3 of *The Kardashians*, Kim read out a long list of things she was looking for in a man. She said her perfect partner should be taller than her, love to work out, be motivated and independent, and have a scent she 'loves', 'even in the gym'. She also wanted someone who would do facials and ice baths with her. And someone who would be adaptable and respectful of others 'especially when no one is watching'.[1]

While some of these requirements might speak to initial physical attraction or hint at social status and shared values, for the most part they have nothing to do with the satisfaction you're going to get from your relationship, and none are the essential qualities that we should be looking for in our long-term partners.

In the dating world, it's a fact that things like your looks, your education, your salary and your job can definitely help you find a partner, as these things are still important to people. The degree of this importance will of course vary depending on the individual, but, regardless, these more superficial categories are of high importance to all of us initially. However, I want to emphasise 'initially', as they quickly fade in relevance in long-term relationships. In short-term mating, on the other hand, it's strictly looks that count — it doesn't matter where you work or how educated you are.

Although we are often told that looks shouldn't matter, we have to accept that physical attractiveness is important to most people. Someone might say, 'Looks aren't my thing. It's all about intelligence for me,' and that's valid, but, as we've seen, I still believe that there needs to be a minimum level of physical attractiveness for most of us. It comes back to evolutionary psychology again. There's a reason why we have an interest in what someone looks like: things like the golden mean (see page 95) and symmetry of facial features are built in to our psychology through millions of years of evolution.

But why is social status, as indicated by career, income and education, important? Well, like attractiveness, it goes back to evolution and the earlier, more pragmatic times of mating, as defined by Maslow's hierarchy of needs — in this case safety. If you had a higher position in the social hierarchy during the period when human relationships were developing and becoming more complex, you were less likely to be murdered or enslaved.

Today, there are special privileges for the folks who are at the top of the social totem pole. Who doesn't like having disposable income and the increased access that social status provides? You see this in the persistence of the class system in the UK. It's not always overtly stated, but beneath the surface a lot of the people I have worked with are looking for someone who is from the same class, and people don't like to stretch above or go below their perceived social status. This preference is often referred to as 'assortative mating', whereby individuals tend to choose partners who are similar to themselves.

In many societies, social status is associated with access to resources, power and opportunities, and, from an evolutionary perspective, individuals might therefore be inclined to seek partners within a similar social status due to the potential benefits for themselves and their offspring.

There are several theories that help to explain this phenomenon. For example, resource acquisition theory suggests that individuals are attracted to partners who possess resources and can provide support and security.[2] Then there is parental investment theory. Individuals have a limited amount of time, energy and resources to invest in offspring, so seeking partners with a similar social status might increase the likelihood of shared values, goals and lifestyles, leading to more effective cooperation in child-rearing and greater reproductive success.[3] And social exchange theory emphasises the idea that individuals look for partners who offer comparable social and economic benefits. Choosing a partner within a similar social status can ensure a balanced exchange of resources.[4]

This reluctance to seek partners above or below one's social status is why people with the same perceived mate value have ended up mating with each other throughout history. I say 'perceived', because one person might, for example, assign higher social status to an anti-capitalist environmental activist, whereas someone else might prioritise a conservative hedge-fund manager.

The more superficial categories like attractiveness and social status align with the basic physiological and safety needs at the bottom of Maslow's pyramid. As we go up the pyramid, those higher-level needs, of love and belongingness, and self-esteem, align with the deeper qualities that we're looking for in people as we move towards self-actualisation. This is why those base qualities like attractiveness and social status, while important at the outset, aren't going to help you to sustain a long-term relationship.

So, what are the characteristics that people say they want? My mentor and friend Rachel Greenwald, who is one of the top matchmakers in the world and went to Harvard Business School, has done a lot of studies around this in terms of the characteristics that people profess they want in a potential partner, and kindness continually ranks highly, as does humour. People also say they want someone who is conscientious, dependable and trustworthy. And often people just say that they want someone who is a good person.

What I want to underscore here is that these are the characteristics that we profess to want (I'll get on to what we actually need in a bit). So why is it that we profess to want these things? Well, we have to remember that most of us are coming from trauma and unhealthy relationships in the past, and these things guide what some of us are looking for. Other people just don't know what they want, either because they don't know what would constitute a healthy partner for them or because they haven't given it any real thought. And a lot of people are heavily influenced by culture. For example, they're scrolling through their social media feeds and saying, 'I want a partner who does that.'

As I've said, your partner being physically attractive to you continues to be important, but as you establish a deeper bond emotionally, their attractiveness actually increases. And we think that things like kindness and humour are important because we perceive them to be the things that will help us to connect and bond on that deeper level. Remember, there are three aspects to love: friendship, intimacy and commitment (see page 25). And people think that the higher-level attributes will help to cement those three categories. And they are right — we need to look for the qualities that align with the higher segments of the pyramid and contribute to Carol Ryff's six dimensions of psychological well-being. It's just that there are things we profess to want and then there are things that we need that we're unaware of.

INCONSEQUENTIAL DEAL-BREAKERS

Relationship science shows us the criteria that we should really be applying when looking for long-term partners, which is just as well, as most of us are highly irrational when making decisions of the heart. Love is emotional, but the more you can use the data, the more you can act rationally, the more you can be informed, and the more aware you are, the better you're going to be able to navigate this very difficult emotional landscape. If you're driving to somewhere you've never been before, you don't guess the directions and you don't wear a partial blindfold. You follow Google Maps and make sure your sight is unobscured — that's using the available information and acting rationally.

This is not meant as a criticism, as it's important to reiterate that it is only in recent years that we have begun to learn the criteria. Historically, there hasn't been much research on this topic, and the best evidence has come within the last two to three decades or so. For example, the longest-running study on couples (led by my dear friend Dr Terri Orbuch) was only started in 1986. Hip-hop is older than that. Also, most psychologists were focused on what people prefer in a partner as opposed to what it is that actually sustains a partnership. This is changing, and we now have access to a lot of new research.

A list of requirements is not bad in and of itself, as we do have to come up with criteria in order to be able to judge whether a partner is suitable. But we need to ask ourselves if we have the right criteria and then rationally assess if someone meets those criteria. Most people come up with long lists of requirements and preferences that are not ultimately the ones that are going to help them sustain a long-term relationship — think back to my client and her spreadsheet — and they do this for a range of legitimate reasons. Perhaps you admire Kim Kardashian and want to be like her, so when you see her discussing her list of superficial requirements, you think that's what you should do too. Or perhaps you are buying into outdated concepts, like those put forward by the book *The Rules*.[5]

The main problem, though, is that we are not clear about what we truly need, as opposed to what we want. If Kim Kardashian says she needs a partner to have good teeth rather than just wanting this, it suggests to me that she is being closed-minded in her approach to finding love. And the longer the list you have, the more rigid and closed-minded you likely are.

It's important not to turn your wants into deal-breakers and get hung up on the minutiae. My sense is that people do this because they are trying to determine what they need, but they don't know how to go about it, so they apply quite specific deal-breakers as a kind of substitute. They have watched reality dating shows and listened to friends, and know that criteria are important, but they don't really know what they should be looking for. I think another reason for this is because of all the talk around self-love and self-improvement and self-worth and self-esteem — people have heard these concepts and think the way to achieve them is to have rigid requirements. Then there's the whole movement around not settling. People want to be boss chicks and badasses, which has led to them thinking they need to reject someone who does ninety-nine things right but one thing wrong.

There might also be an element of self-sabotage for some people. Having a long list of superficial requirements and deal-breakers can be a way of avoiding making a connection and being vulnerable, because it is almost

impossible for one person to fulfil every specific requirement that they have. As soon as someone exhibits a
behaviour that doesn't meet their criteria, they can kick
them to the kerb and, by doing so, give in to their fear of
commitment. This is particularly the case for people
with avoidant attachment styles (see page 19).

I have also seen a resurgence in the popularity of
astrology in dating recently. I think the reason for this is
again because people are looking for criteria that will
help them to judge a good match, and they view astrology as another way of quantifying how people show up
in life. The concept of love languages has also become
hugely popular, which again comes down to people
looking for a rational authority outside of themselves
that can help them to navigate the dating environment.
This idea comes from Gary Chapman's book *The 5 Love
Languages*, in which he argues that there are five ways
people can show love: giving gifts, acts of service, words
of affirmation, physical touch and quality time.[6] However, a lot of people misinterpret this concept. Perhaps
they've heard people talk about it on reality TV shows,
so they write in their profiles that they are looking for
someone who has the same love language as they do. But
that's not what Chapman was talking about. He wasn't
saying that two people need to have the same love

language; he was saying that you need to know what your partner's love language is so that you can show them love in a way that they will understand and appreciate. Jill's love language is gifts — if I give her gifts, she feels my love — but mine is acts of service — do something on my behalf and it translates as an act of love in my eyes. It's an interesting concept, but it's misinterpreted and turned into something it's not supposed to be because people are seeking rational methods. Unfortunately, I don't think astrology or love language as marks of compatibility are the answer.

So, if there is a wide range of internal and external forces at play that can lead to us not coming up with good lists of rational requirements, how do we get around that?

If you are looking for a long-term relationship, we now have enough information to establish the important criteria. Much of this data comes from the various marital-satisfaction scales that are used in psychology, such as the Kansas Marital Satisfaction Scale and the Quality of Marriage Index.* These assess things like adaptability, happiness and joy, communication, and the ability to self-express, all of which add up to show

---

* Although these scales were created for married couples, their findings are relevant for all long-term, committed relationships.

what makes for a strong partnership. It is these qualities that drive high satisfaction and should therefore provide the criteria we apply when looking for a partner. More importantly, it is also possible to pinpoint how you can go about determining if your partner has those qualities (which I'll get on to in a moment).

As we've seen, another good way to ensure you are making rational decisions about your love life is to bring in your friends and family. Having an open discussion with the people in your village is something that happened more in the past and still happens in other cultures, and it can be incredibly helpful to get this outside point of view. Of course, the people who are closest to you have a vested interest, so how do you know that they're going to be able to give you an objective opinion? Well, it's probably going to be difficult to secure a 100 per cent unbiased point of view, but the people in your village have your best interests at heart, so at least they're biased in your favour.

Also, I mentioned earlier that we employed 360-degree analysis in our matchmaking agency, and I think this is the most prudent way for you to take in information from your friends and family too. We would never call everybody into a room and ask them to talk about their loved one in front of each other, because this could lead to groupthink. You instead need to talk to people individually to get their feedback, and you need to talk to a range of people. It's also helpful to allow your partner to interact directly with your friends and family. What you're then looking for is consensus.

On *Lorraine*, someone phoned in and asked for my advice about the guy she'd been dating for nine months, because all of her friends hated him. Her question to me was, 'Paul, how can I get them on board to support me?' And my response was, 'If all of the people who care most about you hate him, then it likely means something, even if it's not something that you want to hear.' One person not liking him would have been just one of those things — everyone not liking him was a red flag.

But you can't outsource the decision-making process to your friends and family. They're just a useful source of perspective and opinion, and, ultimately, the decision is yours. Also, people's villages are unfortunately shrinking, so there are fewer options to have these intimate discussions with. This means the more you're able to do it for yourself, the better. That's why being armed with the right information is so important — you are much more likely to make a good, rational decision that will lead to the type of relationship that you really want.

THE FIVE FUNDAMENTALS

So, we've established that it is important to look for what you need rather than what you want in a partner, and that it is vital to approach the selection process rationally, leaning on your village to help you along the way. But what are the fundamental qualities that you should be looking for?

Over my many years in the matchmaking space, my research at Tinder and my work with leading psychologists with expertise in relationship science, I have refined the criteria that I think are essential, settling on a list of five fundamental trait categories that you need in a partner. These are:

1. Emotional fitness
2. Courageous vision
3. Resilient resourcefulness
4. Open-minded understanding
5. Compassionate support

Underpinning the five fundamentals are the right relationship dynamics. These are the same relationship goals, shared values, physical attractiveness/aligned sexual boundaries and genuine interest, which essentially just means that both parties are being sincere in their inter-actions and with their feelings. Relationship dynamics relate to the way you interact as a couple, whereas the five fundamentals describe the characteristics that you need in a partner. Together they can tell you if you could potentially have a high level of satisfaction with some-one in the long term, and whether that person will help you to be your best self.

When looking for a partner, you need someone who either scores highly or is in the process of improving in all five fundamental areas. In other words, they don't have to be perfect when it comes to these criteria. Instead, they have to be at a level that is minimally acceptable to you (which you can use the LRSS at the end of the book to help determine — see page 245). And because these things are all essentially skills, they can be worked on.

Emotional fitness is made up of a number of aspects, the first of which is emotional availability. This comes down to someone's capacity and willingness to engage in emotional connection and expression, with others or themselves. For instance, can they talk about their fears and express their desires? Next is emotional stability, which is arguably less talked about than emotional avail-ability and intelligence but just as important, if not more so. It consists of low neuroticism and not being moody, and indicates a person's ability to restabilise after being agitated or experiencing stress. Finally, you have emotional intelligence, which is how you manage your emotions, coupled with your awareness of and ability to help manage other people's emotions.

Next up is courageous vision, which is a willingness to face your fears coupled with the imagination and bravery to tackle big ideas or challenges. Resilient resourcefulness, meanwhile, is being knocked down, even if you have faced your fears, and getting up again. It's also about having the ability to navigate trials and adapt to changing situations in a practical and resourceful way. Open-minded understanding is characterised by being curious and non-judgemental, leading to an openness to different perspectives and interest in other people and the wider world. It drives active listening, and it has direct links to high rates of marital and relationship satisfaction.[7] Last but not least is compassionate support, which is about being kind, empathetic and encouraging, as well as being able to put someone else's priorities before your own.

The combination of these qualities provides us with all of the traits we need in a partner to have a healthy relationship. So, for example, we know a big issue for couples is conflict resolution[8] – how do you problem-solve when something goes wrong or you disagree? Well, you need emotional intelligence and vision. If it's a bad argument, you need emotional stability and resilience so you can come right back from it. Good communication stems from emotional availability, a lack of judgement, and curiosity. To trust someone is an act of courage. To forgive someone is an act of empathy. Everything that you need for a high-satisfaction relationship stems from these five fundamentals.

One of the criteria that I hear most often from people is that they want someone who makes them laugh. And while humour is important, I'd argue that it is another component of the five fundamentals, as you need to be emotionally available and curious to find someone funny. Studies have shown that you can have a different sense of humour than your partner, but an appreciation of one another's humour is indicative of some level of compatibility.[9] This also hints at another important relationship skill underpinned by the five fundamentals, and that is compromise. You don't need to have the same perspective, but as long as you can compromise, you're going to be able to sustain a relationship. A compromise is basically a form of negotiation, which in turn requires emotional intelligence and kindness. And sex is, of course, a big part of many romantic relationships, but it is of varying importance, and the five fundamentals can all contribute to you having a healthy sex life. For example, the only way to determine how exploratory you are with your sexual habits with your partner is through communication, and to communicate well you need, among other things, emotional intelligence, a lack of judgement, and curiosity.

So, finding a partner who exhibits all five fundamentals to some level is going to greatly enhance your chances of having a loving, satisfied and long-lasting relationship. Beyond that, though, the five fundamentals will also allow you to achieve high levels of psychological well-being, as they all contribute to the six dimensions that are needed for a good life according to Carol Ryff's model. For example, resilient resourcefulness, courageous vision and open-minded understanding include traits that will help you to score highly in the area of personal growth. Similarly, positive relations with others requires emotional fitness, compassionate support and open-minded understanding.

Whereas I spoke earlier about the inconsequential deal-breakers that some of us impose, being deficient in one of these five core criteria is a legitimate reason to discount a potential partner. Someone could have emotional fitness, courageous vision, open-minded understanding and resilient resourcefulness, and be a psychopath completely lacking in compassionate support. That's why you need to see all five to a minimally acceptable level.

IDENTIFYING THE FIVE FUNDAMENTALS

So how can you make sure that the person you are interested in has these qualities, particularly when, outside of Gen Z, you're often meeting someone's representative in the first instance? First, you need to be aware of and really internalise these five fundamentals — tattoo them on your arm if need be! Awareness is the first step to intrinsically understanding that you can't accept less. You need to identify all five.

Second, people can be manipulative, so a longer courtship helps you to get beyond the representative and see someone for who they really are. A study has shown that the divorce rate is lower for people who had an approximately two-year engagement than for those who got married more quickly or after a much longer courtship.[10] The reason for the former is that you need enough time to see your partner in conditions that will test these criteria.

Let's take emotional fitness as an example. Unfortunately, there is a good chance you will lose a family member, or a job, or face another major life challenge, within a roughly two-year timeframe. When Jill and I were dating, I lost my grandfather, and that was truly the moment I knew I had to marry this woman. She dropped everything, drove me almost eight hours to the funeral and stayed with me throughout. You can't create a test. You have to see a person in action, and that usually takes time.

It's also important to look for consistency. This is a big thing when it comes to kindness — does the person turn it on and off? If you look at their pattern of behaviour, you can begin to suss out whether it is an actual characteristic that they have or if it's just a performance.

Holidays are also fantastic testing grounds, because you're outside of your day-to-day environment and are forced to make new decisions together. You can test someone's emotional stability and intelligence, and it can be a good way to see if you are able to resolve conflicts. The first time Jill and I had a real argument was in Disney World, of all places. We were able to communicate our way through it and bounce back quickly, which told us a lot about our compatibility.

The division of labour is another key testing ground, because it's often cited as a reason why relationships fail. It's not about who does what, necessarily — it's about negotiating a fair balance, as this demonstrates your ability to communicate and be kind (see Chapter 9 for more on relationship equity). And you can tell this early on by someone's willingness to help you with everyday tasks like cooking — does the person you are dating offer to help you in the kitchen?

Sex can also tell us a lot about the five fundamentals. I see this on *Married at First Sight* all the time. A couple gets together, and they are having sex like rabbits. Then, when we talk to them, they say, 'The sex is great!' Of course it is — it's the first week! The real test is month seven — how is the sex now? Have you been able to communicate your likes and dislikes? How does your partner respond when you lay out your boundaries? And if you have different libidos, can you negotiate a compromise that works for both people? This is what I mean by having aligned sexual boundaries.

It takes time to connect on a deeper level, and the best sex is when you have the highest level of emotional intimacy with your partner. If you have a partner who exhibits the five fundamentals, I guarantee you're going to have higher levels of emotional intimacy, and your physical intimacy will go through the roof as a result. So, if you're just having sex for the sake of it, it might be fun, but it's not going to tell you anything important about your compatibility with a long-term partner.

Sex aside, rushing into commitment can be dangerous, especially if you base your decision on what you want as opposed to what you need. Say you meet someone who meets all of your superficial requirements and there are no so-called deal-breakers: you might think you've met the love of your life. But, as we've seen, those requirements don't tell you whether you are compatible in the long term, and you haven't been tested yet. If you meet someone who is the right height, doesn't chew with their mouth open and dresses nicely, and you fly to Las Vegas and get married almost immediately, it's likely that it won't be long until you're divorced.

I know this sounds unromantic, but I've never been a believer in love at first sight. I was really convinced, though, by my friend Dr Helen Fisher, one of the foremost authorities in the world on how the brain functions when you're in love. Everything she's taught me suggests that what we have instead is lust at first sight. We can have immediate desire, but love is a function of commitment, which has to play itself out over time. It doesn't have to be commitment for ever, but it does have to be commitment over a significant period.

You can work out the relationship dynamics of mutual physical attraction, genuine interest, goals and values first, because they can be determined quicker than the five fundamentals — mutual physical attraction takes milliseconds.[11] Of course, goals and values are partly judged by what someone professes to you, and obviously people can be disingenuous, so you still want to keep an eye on this over time, but you can ascertain whether there is compatibility in this regard from the outset. That's why the relationship goals feature, for example, is so popular on Tinder. And although our values show up in our actions, you can determine those more quickly than, say, assessing someone's courageous vision, which is more likely going to take a longer period to see play out. That said, you can still look for signs of the five fundamentals from the outset — for instance, if someone is listening to you, this suggests they have the traits that characterise open-minded understanding.

So, I'm not saying you have to be with someone for two years until you know for sure — you can pull the plug at any point if you realise that the relationship dynamics are off or one of the five fundamentals is missing, because all are required to some degree.

Last but not least, you can use the LRSS at the end of the book (see page 245) to help you frame your thinking about whether or not the right relationship dynamics are in place and if the person you are dating exhibits the five fundamentals to some level. We have also built in a way to check if your judgement is being clouded by infatuation, which is a sure-fire way to let emotion override reason.

♥

The beauty of the five fundamentals is that they are not only important for romantic relationships; they apply to friendships and even business partnerships too. And all the qualities you want in somebody else, you should have as well. You should have compassionate support and courageous vision and open-minded understanding and resilient resourcefulness and emotional fitness. If you do and you meet someone who has these qualities too, you will have an excellent chance of going the distance and having a meaningful relationship that lasts, and you will also be ideally placed to realise your best self.

KEY TAKEAWAYS

1. Many of us think we know what we want, but in the process of defining our criteria we impose unhelpful and restrictive deal-breakers.

2. It's important to make rational decisions and look for what you need in a partner rather than what you think you want.

3. The key components of lasting compatibility are the right relationship dynamics and the five fundamentals: emotional fitness, courageous vision, resilient resourcefulness, open-minded understanding and compassionate support.

'TRUST YOUR INSTINCTS,
VALUE YOUR SELF-WORTH
AND REFUSE TO SETTLE
FOR ANYTHING LESS THAN
YOU DESERVE'

8

RED FLAGS: HOW TO IDENTIFY TOXIC PARTNERS

In the previous chapter, we looked at the five fundamentals that you should be looking for in a partner. However, as I mentioned, these aren't absolutes, and everyone has different priorities. If we think in terms of the LRSS at the end of the book (page 245), one person could score highly on compassionate support and another could have a relatively low score. As long as they have some level of this fundamental, along with some level of the four others, there is something to work on, and it really comes down to what is acceptable and attractive to each individual.* As we also saw, it will probably take you a

---

* There are certain low-level scores on the assessment tool we've created that suggest a partner is not viable for a long-term relationship. However, if that partner works on developing the areas they're weaker in, they will become stronger as a partner.

bit of time until you are able to work out to what degree a potential partner exhibits the five fundamentals, which is absolutely fine — you can't always have all of the answers up front.

This doesn't mean that there aren't situations in which you need to walk away quickly, though. In this chapter, I'm going to tell you about the personality traits that are unacceptable no matter what. You can't engage in a healthy relationship with a person who exhibits one of these traits, as it is guaranteed to be toxic, and your well-being — emotional, psychological and/or physical — will be directly threatened by that toxicity.

One of the main problems is that these are the folks we often find to be more attractive and who tend to do better on the dating scene. This is why it's so important to be aware of who they are so you can protect yourself from these members of what has been referred to as the dark tetrad of personality traits: narcissism, psychopathy, Machiavellianism and sadism.

I first came across what was then referred to as the dark triad in David Buss's book *Bad Men*,[1] but the concept was originally coined in a 2002 paper by Delroy Paulhus and Kevin Williams, in which they discussed narcissism, psychopathy and Machiavellianism, and pointed out how dangerous someone could be if they had all of those qualities.[2] They also observed that many of the character-istics of these traits are similar: a narcissist, a psychopath and a Machiavellian all lack empathy to varying degrees. A few years later, other researchers argued that sadism was closely linked to the original dark-triad traits — sadists also lack empathy, for example — hence why I choose to refer to the dark tetrad here.

David Buss's research has shown that there is a cor-relation between the success of mate selection and the dark tetrad, with people who score highly when it comes to these behaviours proving to be great at short-term mating and terrible at long-term mating. This is why it's so important to weed out these people — they are not suitable as long-term partners and are more often than not going to lead to toxic relationships.

THE DARK TETRAD

NARCISSISM

Narcissism is an excessive regard for oneself, whether that is physical appearance or other abilities, such as intelligence. During one of my chats with Dr Angela Smith, she provided me with a great analogy for narcis-sism in dating: if a narcissist goes to a coffee shop and orders a coffee, it will be pleasurable to them in the moment, but as soon as it is finished, they'll throw the empty cup away and not think twice about it. You are the coffee in this scenario — once a narcissist is done with you, they won't give you another moment's thought.

Narcissistic personality disorder (NPD) is a clinically diagnosed mental health condition characterised by a pervasive pattern of grandiosity, a need for admiration and a lack of empathy. However, it is important to distinguish between clinical and subclinical narcissism, as they represent different levels of severity and impairment. Clinical narcissism refers to individuals who meet the criteria outlined in the *Diagnostic and Statistical Manual of Mental Disorders*, the main resource for the diagnosis and treatment of mental disorders in the USA.[3] These individuals exhibit a pervasive pattern of narcissistic traits that significantly impact their daily functioning and relationships. Diagnosis is typically made by a qualified mental health professional using a comprehensive assessment and evaluation. The criteria include having an exaggerated sense of self-importance and superiority, preoccupation with fantasies of unlimited success, power, brilliance or beauty, a belief in their own specialness and a need for excessive admiration, a sense of entitlement and an expectation of favourable treatment, exploitative behaviour and a lack of empathy, being envious of others or believing others are envious of them, and arrogant and haughty behaviours or attitudes.

Subclinical narcissism, on the other hand, refers to narcissistic traits in individuals who do not meet the full criteria for a clinical diagnosis. These individuals might exhibit some narcissistic characteristics, but the impact on their functioning and relationships is less severe. Subclinical narcissism can manifest in various ways, such as a tendency to seek attention and validation from others, an inflated sense of self-importance and a need for admiration (but not to the extent seen in clinical narcissism), some exploitative or entitled behaviours, and occasional lack of empathy or difficulty understanding others' perspectives. It is worth noting that subclinical narcissism is not considered a diagnosable mental health disorder. However, it can still have implications for individuals' interpersonal relationships and overall well-being, albeit to a lesser extent than clinical narcissism.[4]

This demonstrates that narcissism exists on a continuum, and it's therefore important to acknowledge that it can sometimes be a positive thing; for example, it can be a factor in someone being successful and attractive. Over my years of working on dating shows, many of the contestants have scored slightly higher on the scale of narcissism than the average person, although not to the point that they would be considered clinical narcissists. As a matter of fact, it's to your advantage to test higher in this context, as you need to stand out from the crowd (see Chapter 6). Entrepreneurs also tend to test higher on the narcissism scale than the average person, because what they do is partly about being able to sell a vision and having a high level of self-esteem. So, there are some positives to exhibiting a degree of narcissism. The problem is when you tip over and use everyone to your advantage. That's when you become the ultimate user and abuser. Recognising when you get to that tipping point is the difficult thing (I go into this in more detail later in the chapter).

PSYCHOPATHY

Psychopathy, meanwhile, essentially comes down to not feeling empathy. Different to narcissism, it is only clinically diagnosed, but there is still a spectrum — it's just a much shorter spectrum. And, unfortunately, a psychopath is someone who can do extremely well on the dating scene. Research has shown, for example, that narcissists and psychopaths have the most success at speed dating.[5] Because a psychopath has zero empathy, they'll tell you absolutely anything. In other words, they're very proficient at lying, and they don't tend to have any of the tells that come with someone who's not familiar with lying, so it's very hard to spot their deception.

Again, similarly to narcissists, psychopaths tend to invest more in how they look, which is important when we are looking for a short-term mate, and they are great at small talk and illuminating their social status, which are more reasons why we can sometimes be attracted to them. Having no empathy for anyone else and only caring about what they want can also come across as them being strong and having their crap together. In other words, they can present as supremely confident, which can sometimes be an attractive quality.

SADISM

A sadist is someone who derives pleasure from other people's pain. When I was little, a kid in our neighbourhood would use a magnifying glass to burn insects. That was someone exhibiting the signs of sadism at an early age. In a dating context, a sadist might be someone who takes pleasure in humiliating their partner in public. The key thing with a sadist is that they cause you pain directly and deliberately. A narcissist might also cause you pain, but they are doing this as a by-product of their behaviour without thinking about how it impacts you. Sadism is no longer considered to be a clinical pathology and is instead categorised as a person-ality trait.

MACHIAVELLIANISM

Machiavellianism, meanwhile, has come to describe cal-culated risk-taking, manipulation, coercion and clever but dishonest strategising, and is named after the Renais-sance political theorist Niccolò Machiavelli. I first became aware of him when I read his book *The Prince*[6] shortly after I graduated from university, and then in a dating context when he was referenced in Robert Greene's book *The Art of Seduction*.[7] Again, it is a personality trait rather than something that is diagnosed clinically.

The dating and matchmaking industries have to take some responsibility for the rise of Machiavellianism in a relationship context, because we're always recommend-ing strategies. Here are the rules. Here are the ten steps. One of the biggest inflection points in the dating space was when Neil Strauss wrote the book *The Game* in 2005, which he has since distanced himself from.[8] This was what really led to the rise of so-called pick-up artistry and other dark, underground strategies, mostly geared towards short-term mating.

A Machiavellian takes pleasure from game playing, with its focus on self-interest and stroking the ego — for example, the person who's at a bar with their friends and says, 'You know what, I have no interest in that person over there, but I bet I can get them to buy me a drink.' It's about them making themselves feel good by manipulating someone else. This is ultimately about the Machiavellian's low self-esteem. And there is a lack of morality if they're willing to prioritise their personal game over the suffering of others.

All of the dark-tetrad traits are part genetic and part learned. Where the dividing line lies is not clear, but the learned part starts with attachment (see page 18). Most members of the dark tetrad are, as you would probably guess, anxious or avoidant. And socialisation throughout their years shapes these qualities further. For example, a lot of the learned aspect of these malevolent behaviours is rooted in trauma.

My childhood neighbour with the magnifying glass was in part influenced by societal pressures too. The reflex response of a group of little boys who witness that kind of cruelty is likely to be, 'That's so cool.' But I knew it wasn't cool, because when I went home and told my mum what had happened, she said, 'That's terrible,' and explained to me why what he'd done was unacceptable. This is where parenting, love and community shape what someone perceives to be acceptable or not. One of my other friends might have gone home and received no response or have been told that it was an OK thing to do.

In terms of prevalence, narcissism is between 1 and 15 per cent of the US population and growing,[9] Machiavellianism is up to 16 per cent of the population and growing[10] and sadism and psychopathy are low, at less than 1 per cent of the population.[11] Within that there could of course be overlaps. And these numbers only capture the people who've passed the threshold of each of the individual traits. But you could have someone who scores fairly high on the narcissism scale but is not yet considered to be a narcissist and does not therefore count towards the 1–15 per cent figure. The same goes for the Machiavellian group. And there are probably a significant number of people who test highly for both narcissism and Machiavellianism without fully qualifying.

David Buss has written about the dark tetrad becoming more prevalent among men. The exception to this is Machiavellianism, which is seen at a higher rate in women, at least in a professional context.[12] I think this is mainly due to the elevation of women in society. Women are now competing to a higher degree in the workplace, and there's more competition between the sexes in education, politics and even the domestic sphere that weighs dramatically on how and why they show up. The perception that there's a smaller pool of available men also drives this trend for more gameplaying by women in the dating world. And then there are all of the shows and magazines that promote strategising and manipulation when it comes to finding a partner. But narcissism, psychopathy and sadism are more prevalent in men.[13]

This all goes to show that this is a massive issue and something to be taken seriously. The term 'narcissist', for instance, is often thrown about and not assessed with any rigour. The risk is that this diminishes the truth of what an actual narcissist is, which is very dangerous. That's why it is also important that I stress that we're talking about the clinical definitions of these words rather than those more colloquial definitions − for example, calling someone who is a bit vain a narcissist.

THE DANGERS OF THE DARK TETRAD IN A RELATIONSHIP

I mentioned previously that people who exhibit dark-tetrad qualities can sometimes be attractive, especially in a short-term context. This is because they present as being confident, smooth and physically attractive, and as having high social status. The dark tetrad therefore feed those superficial things that we look for in short-term relationships and fulfil those base needs, but if you want a long-term partnership that moves you closer to self-actualisation and a high score on Carol Ryff's PWB scale, there's a deficit, because these people don't have the depth. We might have evolved and been socialised to look for characteristics such as physical attractiveness, but you need to reprogram your mind and look for the five fundamentals instead (see Chapter 7). By omission, you will then avoid these dark qualities, because someone can't be emotionally fit *and* be in the dark tetrad. That fundamental alone negates all of these negative characteristics.

Jealousy, coerciveness and cruelty, and all of the other damaging traits that you would associate with a bad partner, feed into the four headline categories. And if you end up with someone who falls into one of these categories, you are at risk of emotional, physical and psychological abuse. It's likely that they will try to exploit or demean you, damaging your self-esteem and exerting control over your thoughts and emotions. The chances are they will lack empathy and not provide you with any emotional support — they're not going to be there when you are struggling, and you need your partner to help you. A relationship with them is likely to be characterised by constant manipulation and deception — they're going to lie to you in order to achieve their own goals and maintain power in the relationship. The dynamic is always going to feel unbalanced, which will put you constantly on guard as the weaker, more vulnerable party. This can lead to you walking on eggshells the entire time. There are probably going to be high levels of conflict as well, with lots of arguments and little resolution. And last but not least, there is the potential for physical harm. Some combination of these things is almost guaranteed if you enter a relationship with someone in the dark tetrad.

In addition, the people who exhibit these qualities don't take responsibility themselves and always shift the blame on to their partners, making them feel like they are responsible for the other person's shortcomings. Or if not their partners, they shift the blame on to anyone else but themselves — friends, family, even children in more established relationships. This makes the cycle even more difficult to break because you are made to feel that you are to blame. We hear this in the most extreme instances, such as domestic abuse: 'He hit me because I deserved it.'

Jealousy is often mentioned as being one of the biggest problems in a partner. But it's not a deal-breaker in the same way that someone who's a full-blown narcissist or sadist is a deal-breaker. Jealousy might be a feature of narcissism in some people, but you can learn to become less jealous. For example, a partner who doesn't exhibit jealousy and has a secure attachment style can help you to be less jealous. Dr Angela Smith explained to me that a full-blown narcissist, on the other hand, is always going to be a narcissist. It's never a question of whether they can change. You just have to decide if you are willing to put up with the fact that this is who they are — and I'd suggest you shouldn't.

A common refrain in the world of dating is, 'I can change my partner for the better. I can work on their flaws and make them what I want them to be.' I'm not sure wanting to change someone is necessarily always a positive thing, but what I do know is that you can't change someone who is a fully paid-up member of the dark tetrad. That's why they are so dangerous. A lot of people might think that they could handle a Machiavellian manipulator, for example, but I disagree, because their manipulation links to everything. How are you ever going to be able to trust what they say to you? It could always be a manipulation to get their own way. It's difficult to be in a healthy partnership with someone like this, and a toxic relationship with that person is much more likely.

Similarly, I hear a lot of people in toxic relationships say that they want to talk to their partner so that they can work it out. Unfortunately, if your partner is a member of the dark tetrad, you can never work it out. And that might be acceptable to you if you are just looking for a short-term partner who fulfils your most basic needs and you are not interested in a deeper, more meaningful relationship. For everyone else, a member of the dark tetrad is to be avoided at all costs, and if you come to the realisation that you are in a relationship with someone like that, you need to create your plan of departure and then execute it.

IDENTIFYING THE DARK-TETRAD QUALITIES IN A POTENTIAL PARTNER

So, how you spot these negative qualities and prevent yourself from being fooled into thinking they're something else — like confidence, for instance — is the big-money question. The first thing you need to do — and you're already doing it by reading this book — is to educate yourself; awareness and knowing what to look out for and avoid is half the battle.

Next, you need to look at your immediate safety. This is vital. I receive a lot of messages from women who say things like, 'I've been dating this guy for three months, and he got really angry last night. He didn't hit me, but he broke a hole in the wall.' My immediate response is, 'Do you feel safe with this person?' Typically, the answer is, 'Well, most of the time, but not in that moment.' That's a huge problem because there shouldn't ever be a moment when you don't feel safe with your partner. If you start a relationship with someone and you don't feel safe, you have to leave it immediately.

You can also lean on the external observations of your friends and family, which can be extremely telling when it comes to identifying a member of the dark tetrad. As I've said before, you're not always going to be rational when it comes to love, so outside opinions can be helpful for recognising if your potential partner is exhibiting dark-tetrad traits. But in order for this feedback to be valuable, it's important to disclose everything when you're engaging with your friends and family. There is often a tendency to leave out details — using the example above, a lot of people might tell a friend that their partner was angry but leave out the fact that he punched a hole in the wall.

If you feel unsafe with a partner or are a victim of domestic abuse and feel scared or unsure about speaking out, it is crucial to seek help and support from resources that can provide you with guidance, safety planning and assistance. A list of organisations you can go to has been included in the resources section at the end of the book (see page 261).

When consulting your village, it's again important to look for consensus. Typically, you'll hear clues that add up to tell you if the person you're dating is to be avoided. For example, say you bring the person over to meet your mother, go for brunch with them and some friends, and take them to after-work drinks with your co-workers, and you keep hearing something like, 'They seem like a really ambitious person,' you need to dig in and work out what that actually means. Does it suggest they are cut-throat and only focused on themselves? In this way, you can begin to unpack their behaviours based on these consensus points.

'Do I feel supported and encouraged by my partner?' is also an important question to ask yourself, as it speaks to someone's emotional fitness. If this is missing, it might be an indication that the person lacks empathy to a dangerous degree. Inconsistent behaviour can also be a giveaway, as is how someone talks about people in their past. As I said, people in the dark tetrad always assign blame elsewhere and are never accountable — it was always the partner who was at fault, or the situation.

Ultimately, you have to spend enough time with these people to recognise them for who they really are, because they are masters of deception, particularly in the short term. It is only over time that you will begin to see their representative fade away, which is why it sometimes takes as long as two years to get a true sense of who someone really is and whether they are compatible with you. It's even more difficult when you are online, as it is easier to lie when you have the cover of the internet. That's why awareness of these qualities is so important, as it means you are more likely to pick up quite subtle hints, and the earlier you can identify that someone is a member of the dark tetrad and the relationship is therefore not going to work, the better.

Unfortunately, you are in harm's way as long as you're with someone like this. That could be physical harm, but it could also be psychological and emotional. Say you are someone who has a secure attachment style. If you enter a relationship with someone who's a full-blown member of the dark tetrad, there's a good chance you are going to become insecure over time, and all of the great grounding that you've had, and the resolution of trauma that you've done, can be completely unravelled in a couple of months with a really bad person. That's another reason to be aware and to be cautious, and to get out quickly when you see these signs. In a situation like this, you could end up causing extreme trauma that's going to have an impact on every other relationship that you have further down the road. It could even have an impact on your unborn children if you decide to have them. It's that important.

This is why you have to end a relationship with someone like this as soon as possible. Better still, if you are able to recognise these qualities in someone, you need to prevent yourself from getting mixed up with them in the first place. I of course realise that it's not always as simple as just leaving, especially if a relationship is more established. Leaving could cause even more emotional or physical harm to you or to a loved one, at least in the short term. You might not be financially able to do it. You could be physically isolated because you've moved to another country and your visa status is dependent on that person. But the bottom line is that you have to leave. I'll go into this in more detail in a later book in the series, but the moment you know that you're in a relationship with someone who is exhibiting these traits, you have to talk to someone. Being able to express how you feel to someone who's rational is very important. Just that expression alone is going to be therapeutic for you.

Some of what I've talked about in this chapter might sound quite black-and-white, but I also realise that there will often be a fair amount of uncertainty. Perhaps you think someone's a bit of a narcissist, or they have done something cruel and you suspect they might be a sadist, but you're not sure. The question then becomes: how do you gain the certainty that you need to discount someone as a long-term partner or end a fledgling relationship?

As I mentioned before, you would for the most part need to test someone to be certain they fell into one of these categories. But if you see enough indicators line up, it gives you a high degree of confidence that someone could fit into one of the dark-tetrad categories. And regardless of whether someone is a full-blown sadist or clinical psychopath, you shouldn't be in any relationship in which you feel unsafe.

I want to give you the knowledge and awareness of the issues, but you ultimately have to judge for yourself, with the help of your village, whether someone you are interested in has the potential to be a member of the dark tetrad. Yes, this is more difficult when you're dating and not in a relationship yet, but in my experience, people are actually very intuitive about this sort of thing, and when they say, 'Something doesn't feel right,' it is generally because there is a genuine problem.

Another challenge is that one of the main pieces of advice that I'm giving you in this book is that you need to be open-minded and not rush to judgement about someone, particularly if you're aiming for a long-term relationship. But at the same time, you also need to be wary of ending up in a situation with someone like this. To balance those two different approaches, you need to be highly observant and analytical, which is not always easy when it comes to love.

When most people begin to date someone, for the first couple of months they just want to go out and do cool stuff together. Let's go to the park. Let's go rock climbing. Let's go to this restaurant. Let's go to this bar. Generally, there is no rigour as to what you are learning about the other person. Instead, try asking, 'How can I use every interaction to assess whether this person is a good fit for me?' This probably sounds extremely unromantic. It shouldn't, though, because as you learn more about your partner, you should actually feel a deeper connection to them. (The questions in the LRSS on page 245 are also great for this because if you familiarise yourself with the questions, you can begin to ask yourself them as you spend time with your partner.)

If you constantly observe and assess and bring intentionality to the dating process, instead of just leaving it to chance, the good and bad traits will unveil themselves — whether someone is compassionately supportive or self-absorbed, resiliently resourceful or lacking in empathy, emotionally fit or cruel. As you're doing this, you're interacting with the more rational group of friends and family, and bouncing opinions back and forth, which helps to sharpen your observational skills. In this way, you can be open-minded and analytical at the same time. You do, however, need to go diligently through the process. It's another example of using the evidence and data to counterbalance the more emotional and so-called romantic aspects of love that probably come a bit more naturally to most of us.

You might read this chapter and think, 'Wow, there are a lot of bad people out there.' Or you might feel overwhelmed by the presence of toxic people when dating, which is a completely natural reaction. However, I invite you to shift your perspective and embrace a more empowering outlook. Consider this: the majority of people in this world are inherently good, and they embody kindness, empathy and respect in their interactions. This realisation can unleash a powerful sense of optimism.

Rather than dwelling on the negative, let this understanding motivate you to seek out positive connections. Trust what you're learning in this book and your ability to attract individuals who appreciate and uplift you. You deserve relationships that nurture your well-being and growth. While past experiences might have left their mark, they do not define your future. Each encounter serves as a lesson, guiding you towards wiser choices and healthier boundaries. So approach your journey forward with renewed confidence and optimism, and believe in your strength and resilience as you navigate the path ahead. Embrace the belief that you can create relationships filled with joy, support and mutual respect. Trust your instincts, value your self-worth and refuse to settle for anything less than you deserve. Yes, there are people out there whom you need to avoid, but thankfully there are far more who could be just the person you're looking for.

KEY TAKEAWAYS

1. Narcissism, psychopathy, Machiavellianism and sadism — together the dark tetrad of personality traits — are genuine deal-breakers.

2. Being in a relationship with someone who exhibits dark-tetrad characteristics can lead to emotional, physical and psychological abuse, and should be avoided at all costs.

3. But don't worry: the majority of people are good, and there are signs you can look out for to help you to discount people with dark-tetrad qualities.

'YOU CAN NEVER HAVE 100
PER CENT CERTAINTY.
THERE'S ALWAYS GOING TO
BE A LEAP OF FAITH'

9

ARE YOU READY FOR FOREVER? UNDERSTANDING THE SIGNS OF COMMITMENT READINESS

We are on the final leg of our journey. Up to this point, I've discussed the importance of doing the work to put yourself in the best position to find love, and I've shown you what is important when it comes to identifying a partner who will give you what you need. The final piece of the puzzle is judging someone's commitment readiness and whether they are the right partner to be with in the long term. If you are ready for a serious relationship but your partner is not prepared or willing to commit, you are setting yourself up for disappointment. Commitment readiness is therefore something you have to determine before you take your relationship to the next stage.

THE COMPONENTS OF COMMITMENT READINESS

So, what do I mean by commitment readiness? Simply put, it is someone showing you they are willing or able to enter into a long-term, committed relationship, whether that be a marriage or some variation of that. In the previous chapter, I explained that a member of the dark tetrad is just not built for the long term, so they are never going to be ready for commitment. But you can also be in a relationship with someone who is not a member of the dark tetrad and who meets all of the five fundamentals but is still not ready.

'My partner is scared of commitment' has become something of a well-trodden cliché, used to mask the fact that maybe someone is just not that into you, but it can be true that someone is fearful of committing to a long-term relationship, or is even unable to. This might be as a result of someone having an avoidant attachment style. Or it could be how they're socialised. Many of us are programmed to be extremely risk-averse. Some people are scared to jump in water, whereas others go on scuba-diving holidays. The difference comes down to how we've been brought up.

Imagine a person growing up in an environment where they witnessed or experienced inconsistent and unstable relationships, or observed their parents or significant adults in their life going through frequent break-ups or divorces. As a result, they might have internalised the message that relationships are inherently unstable and painful. Furthermore, if they were exposed to negative comments like 'marriage is a trap' or 'love only leads to heartbreak', it could further reinforce their fear or scepticism of long-term commitments. And if the person had their own experiences of abandonment or rejection in past relationships, it could further deepen their fear of commitment. For instance, if they were in a relationship in which they felt deeply invested, only to have their partner suddenly leave or betray their trust, it could create a lasting fear of getting hurt again. Over time, these cumulative experiences and messages can shape a person's beliefs and attitudes towards commitment. They can develop a subconscious fear of emotional vulnerability and intimacy, leading to a hesitancy to commit fully or engage in long-term relationships. It should be apparent before you get to the commitment-readiness stage if someone is scared of commitment in this way.

Putting fear to the side, there are four things that I believe underscore commitment readiness, the first of which is trust. This means that you and your partner are able to open up to one another without feeling judged — in essence, your relationship is a safe space. Second is that you have had to resolve conflict more than once. This demonstrates that you have good emotional regulation as a couple and there's active listening that allows you to resolve your differences or negotiate a compromise. Healthy conflict resolution is deciding to deal with your disagreements, rather than sweeping them under the rug, and then moving beyond them once they have been resolved. Number three is simply that you have high relationship satisfaction. You need to find joy in being with your partner.

Last but not least, you can't be of the opinion that there are higher-quality alternative options out there. This is a two-way process: you need to discount the possibility that you could find someone better, as well as being confident that your partner is not going to be looking elsewhere as soon as you commit to one another.

If you enter a relationship with someone who meets all of the criteria I've talked about in this book except for the fact that they believe there are better options available for them, you'll have a fault in your foundation. You can still build a house on that foundation, but there will be a crack that could undermine the integrity of what you have built further down the line. And there's not much you can do about this. The best you can do is be strong in all of the other categories: relationship satisfaction, conflict resolution and trust, with the five fundamentals from Chapter 7 also in place. This gives your relationship a high chance of success. But at the end of the day, if your partner believes that they could find someone better, you are potentially going to be on the chopping block.

That said, while challenging, there are a few indicators that might suggest someone believes they have better alternative options. For example, if someone frequently expresses uncertainty or hesitation about committing to and investing in a romantic relationship, it could be because they are unsure if it is the best choice for them. Or if they actively engage in flirting, dating or keeping their options open, this could indicate that they believe there are more desirable prospects available. Other signs include comparing their current partner to others, or constantly evaluating their partner's qualities and compatibility. And individuals who frequently express dissatisfaction, restlessness or a longing for something more in their relationship might be doing so because they feel unfulfilled and believe that they are settling for less than what they could potentially find elsewhere.

As I've mentioned, people feel like they have more options today than they did twenty years ago. This means that a lot of people are breaking up, whether they're married or not, because they believe that there's someone better out there for them. They're jumping out of relationships not because they can't resolve issues with their partner or have low sexual satisfaction. It's simply that they feel there's a better option. And the more of those higher-quality options they view as being available, the more it decreases their commitment readiness.

There is a bit of 'the grass is always greener' going on here — if you are looking for someone else who is as good or better, there is a danger you're going to miss what is right in front of you. This is because I am talking about the perception of higher-quality alternative options, rather than whether this is actually the case. And unfortunately, it seems to me as though there's a growth in this perception. Psychologically, our ability to assess whether a person is an option for us is not always reliable, so all it takes is for us to believe that we have better options for the decisions we are making to be adversely impacted. In other words, a person's commitment readiness can be influenced whether or not they actually have those options.

You could meet someone fantastic and still have this perception. Take someone who is at the beginning of the dating stage. It's early days and they haven't yet decided whether they're going to be in a committed dating scenario with this particular person. Before long, they ask themselves, 'OK, does this person have what it takes to go long term?' They might have a high level of all the things I've been talking about, and there might still be incredible options available. Those things are not mutually exclusive — sometimes there are better options. You might find someone who is a great candidate for you, but that doesn't mean that they are the only option, because there will always be great people out there. However, once that person enters the beginning of the committed dating phase, that's when they have to resolve these questions. If they are going to commit to someone, perhaps even permanently, they have to believe that person is the best one for them in that particular moment. That's why getting to know someone through the dating process is so important, because you can work out if the person is the strongest match for you. When you decide to commit long-term to someone, you're making a conscious decision to forego those other options.

ASSESSING COMMITMENT READINESS

The process of assessing commitment readiness can start quite early, even from the first time you meet someone. This applies specifically to trust, conflict resolution and high relationship satisfaction.

Then, as you progress, you have to get a real sense that someone is trustworthy. One way to do this is to look for someone who consistently follows through with their responsibilities. And I don't just mean within a relationship — I'm referring to life in general. It could be something as simple as them following through on something they have said they will do. A trustworthy person is someone who is nailing their commitments and responsibilities.

You also need someone who appears to trust you and comes to you in their times of need. They rely on you and give you responsibility in their life. Say you've been dating someone for a couple of months who has a kid and they ask you to pick them up from an after-school club because they are running late — that's a huge sign of trust.

Next is this question of being able to open up without fear of judgement. You sometimes see partners use information in a conflict that was provided in a moment of emotional intimacy. That's a massive red flag that undermines trust by suggesting they've been judging you all along.

A lot of us feel like our intuition is broken, but I think most of us have good intuition when it comes to trust. If you doubt you can trust someone, it's probably for a good reason. And the opposite is true too: if you feel like you can trust someone, it's probably because you can.

There also needs to be an early sign that there's going to be common ground when it comes to conflict resolution. And there are lots of little indicators that, taken together, will give you a strong sense of not only your partner's ability to resolve conflict, but your mutual ability to resolve conflict as a couple — for instance, an ability to compromise on the small things and resolve an issue or negotiate a middle ground in the moment. Negotiations happen all day every day in relationships. I really want to have sushi for dinner but my wife wants to have jerk chicken — how do we negotiate that difference?

Emotional regulation is another great sign that someone will be able to resolve conflict. If you are able to regulate your emotions in the midst of disagreement, you can listen and really hear what is being said. Respecting your boundaries and not continuously trying to push you beyond them is also a good indicator. I see this all the time on the first and second dates. A woman might say, 'I have to be done by ten because I've got work tomorrow.' When it gets closer to 10pm, the date says, 'Let's just go for drinks afterwards.' She drew her line and told you what her boundary was, and it wasn't because she thought you were an asshole — she drew the line there because she has to go to work the next day. This in some ways innocuous comment hints at pushiness and the fact that maybe he's not listening to you. That's why active listening is also very important. Often when we're listening, it's just sound hitting our eardrums, but if someone really hears what you're saying, they can respond critically to what you've said, and add value by making a pertinent comment or asking a searching question. It is also a key component of successful conflict resolution.

Relationship satisfaction is more difficult at the outset, but even then you can begin to get a sense of whether someone is going to bring you happiness if they share the same values as you. And one of the best indicators of high relationship satisfaction is adjustment — in other words, how flexible is your partner in being able to adjust to your schedule and needs? Let's say you and your partner have planned to go out for dinner and a movie on a Friday night. However, during the week leading up to the date, you unexpectedly receive a work assignment with a tight deadline and you find yourself overwhelmed with the workload. You communicate your situation honestly to your partner, expressing your regret that you might not be able to make it to the date as planned. In response, your partner shows understanding and flexibility. Instead of being upset or disappointed, they suggest an alternative plan. They propose coming over to your place, cooking you dinner and then leaving. This would give you the space and time you need to focus on your work. Their proposal has also made it clear that they value spending time with you, regardless of the setting, and want to accommodate your needs and schedule. Their willingness to adjust the plans and prioritise your well-being demonstrates their consideration and adaptability.

Also, do you feel energised or drained when you're with your partner? This is very important. If you think, 'I love being with my partner, but, gosh, he drains me,' well, that's a problem. You should really be thinking, 'I love being around my partner — I feel full of energy,' especially at the outset of a relationship. And do you feel like you can experience new things with your partner? Or when you want to do something novel, would you rather do it on your own?

These things are then tested more fully during the extended courtship period. It's during this time that you can flush out someone's commitment readiness. It's only through someone's actions that you'll be able to tell if they're really ready to commit.

The two-year time period that we discussed in Chapter 7 is applicable again here, but it's just a rule of thumb. You might take longer to get to the point of commitment, or it might be quicker. In general, however, the less time you spend with someone, the higher likelihood there will be issues in your relationship further down the line, because you haven't had enough time to vet your partner properly.

It's also true that you can leave it too long. If your partner is not ready to commit after spending many years together, then they probably won't ever be ready, so there's no point plucking up the confidence to tell them they need to get commitment-ready. It's really just common sense — you need to give it enough time to get to know one another and make a proper assessment, but if you give it too long, you might miss the moment.

Over the course of your courtship, you might have only one or two moments of severe adversity, so you won't know if they can resolve conflict and exhibit low neuroticism and bounce back from the stress and not push your boundaries until you're in the moment. That's the only way to know for sure. They can talk as much as they want. They can show you all of the communication books they've read, but until you're in the moment, you won't know.

The longer you're with someone, the better you'll know them, and the better you'll understand whether you will work in the long term. Part of the reason for this is that what you are ultimately looking for is consistency, not perfection. We're all human, after all. I've missed taking out the rubbish from time to time. The question is: do you have more good days than bad? Is the person you are interested in consistently showing that they embody these characteristics? To reiterate, we're not looking for perfection. We're looking for an indication that someone's moving in the right direction or has these base qualities. If you set the bar too high, no one can get over it.

THE THREE ASPECTS OF A SUCCESSFUL LONG-TERM RELATIONSHIP

If you have the five fundamentals and good relationship dynamics, and you are ready to commit to someone, and they are ready to commit too, you have ticked all of the boxes of compatibility, and you're ready to go. You couldn't have a stronger foundation to embark on a long-term relationship. However, you still need to build a strong relationship on top of that foundation and to do so requires three things that I consider essential for a successful long-term partnership.

The psychologist John Gottman has spent his career studying relationships, specifically marriages, and he has designed models that can predict whether a couple is going to break up.[1] In order to pin down the behaviours that contribute to a relationship failing, he came up with the concept of what he called the 'Four Horsemen': defensiveness, stonewalling, criticism and contempt. Of these four, you could argue that contempt is the most serious, because it ultimately means disrespect, but none are conducive to a happy relationship.

Typically, you don't start off in a relationship with someone who exhibits these behaviours towards you — they build over time, particularly criticism and contempt. However, if the horsemen show up, it is a good sign that the relationship is not going to go the distance.

Next is equity theory, which originated in economics in the 1960s but has been used to analyse intimate relationships too.[2] At its most basic, it describes how individuals seek fairness and balance in their relationships. You could have one partner who is a creative and doesn't have a full-time schedule and one who has more of a standard nine-to-five-type job. Both have been working, but if one doesn't feel that the other is making a fair contribution to the relationship, there is likely going to be a problem. And fair doesn't necessarily mean equal, as long as both people feel as though the other is giving their all.

You hear the question of equity come up all the time in relationship breakdowns. One of the partners says that the other doesn't do anything any more, and that they put all of the effort into looking after their family, for example. To have a partnership that can go long-term, there needs to be equity.

Last but not least, many of us want to feel like we're on the pathway to self-actualisation, have high levels of psychological well-being and can say, 'As a result of being in this relationship, I feel like I am becoming my best self.' In this day and age, when our romantic partners fulfil so many of our needs, this is incredibly important for lots of people, although it is of course absolutely fine if you have different relationship goals.

So, no sign of the Four Horsemen showing up, feeling like you have equity in the relationship and a sense that you are both on the pathway to self-actualisation (if that's what you're aiming for) are the ingredients of a strong long-term relationship once you've picked the right partner. In addition, having a shared vision for the future is also important, especially as it changes over time. Your goals have to evolve with one another. This is actually one of the leading causes of divorce.[3] It's quite common for couples who have children to get to the empty-nest stage and look at one another and think, 'What the hell — I don't even know you any more,' because their goals have diverged. To avoid this, consistent and open communication, and regularly discussing individual aspirations and dreams while cultivating shared interests and goals can help to maintain a strong connection throughout a relationship. Additionally, participating in hobbies or travelling together can foster renewed understanding and create new memories. Ultimately, couples who want to go the distance should prioritise spending quality time together, and actively listening to and supporting one another's growth.

A LEAP OF FAITH

The assessments that I have been talking about in this chapter don't happen in isolation — you need to discuss these things with your partner too. But the reality is, very few couples talk about this stuff before they commit to one another. There's no meaningful discussion around whether they are ready for one another. But everything I've talked about in this book doesn't happen in a vacuum. There's no point in someone reading all of this and doing all this work and identifying all of these qualities in a person and then not communicating with them. It's not a solitary process.

One of the reasons some of us find talking about commitment difficult is that we are worried we might push the other person away. It might be the first time you have been in love, or you might be falling in love again after a difficult previous relationship, both of which scenarios can be scary. That's why it is so critical to be confident and show up and assert yourself and say, 'These are my standards. I need to have a partner who is ready to commit with me.'

Part of being confident is checking in with your values and reminding yourself who you are. What's your rulebook for life? Why are you living the way that you live? What are you here for? This process helps you to boost your self-worth and self-esteem too. You also need to work on your communication and especially your assertiveness, both of which you can practise in other aspects of your life aside from your romantic relationships. And by assertiveness, I don't mean nastiness. I simply mean getting to the point and being confident to say what you want. Some people might think this is a cop-out, but a very effective interim step towards being able to express yourself in this way is writing down your thoughts in a letter to your partner.

Next, you need to focus on your self-care and your support system, both of which are incredibly important when it comes to confidence. Self-care is essentially about recharging your self-esteem and your self-love, which you need if you are to be confident. And finally, start with baby steps. My confidence has always grown when I've been able to look back and see that I took a step and didn't fall.

Ultimately, confidence is what's required to show up and make this extremely big decision, perhaps the most important decision you can make, to commit to a life with someone. And this is doubly scary, because you can never have 100 per cent certainty. There's always going to be a leap of faith. Before you do a skydive, you are bound to be nervous, even if you've done all the training and the equipment has been checked and then checked again. It's not until the moment you jump that you are able to stop worrying and look around and realise how cool it is. This fear is a natural part of life — it's millions of years of natural selection trying to protect us from something that might potentially hurt us. The reason why it is so scary to commit to someone is because you're taking your heart and you're handing it over to someone and you're saying, 'Please don't crush it.' But ultimately you have little control over someone's ability to hurt you, and that is scary.

But getting to the point that you want to spend the rest of your life with someone is also the best thing in the world, with seemingly unlimited ways of making your life better. Even before you get to that stage, the concepts in this book are positioned to help you to become the best version of yourself and, by doing so, you'll be in the strongest position to find love. That's essentially what this book is about — becoming the best version of you, before and during a relationship. In fact, there's value in doing the work I've outlined in the book regardless of whether you find love or not. And that applies to everyone: men, women, non-binary people, straight, bisexual, gay, polyamorous, and so on. This book was not written with one particular gender or persuasion in mind.

Now that I've shared with you my insights and expertise, the next step is to go out and put some of the advice into practice. The good news is that you will be much better equipped to navigate the world of dating and find love than you were. To really press home this advantage,

I would recommend that you go back and reread the key takeaways at the end of each chapter and identify if there's anything that you don't fully understand or need to work on further. You can then use the information in that chapter to further absorb the recommendations that I am making. You can also use the LRSS that follows. There is a version of the scale on my website (paulcbrunson.com) that you can fill out too, along with additional resources to help you in your search for love. Of course, once you've found love, you need to know how to keep it, so watch out for the next book in the series, which will tell you all you need to know about what makes a successful relationship last.

As I said at the beginning, I realise that finding a partner who is right for you can be daunting, but I am confident that the person you have been looking for is waiting to be found. All you need to do is keep the faith and approach your search with a bit more intention and a little less emotion, and I know you will be successful.

KEY TAKEAWAYS

1. Before making the decision to embark on a long-term relationship with someone, you need to assess the four elements of commitment readiness: trust, effective conflict resolution, high relationship satisfaction and not thinking there are better options available.

2. Three things are needed to make a relationship work in the long term: no sign of the 'Four Horsemen' — defensiveness, stonewalling, criticism and contempt — relationship equity and feeling like you are on the path to being your best self.

3. You need to discuss all of this with your partner before you commit to a long-term relationship, which takes assertiveness and courage.

THE LONG-TERM RELATIONSHIP SATISFACTION SCALE (LRSS)

This tool is designed to support you in making wise choices when it comes to selecting a partner for a lasting relationship. Whether you wish to assess your current relationship or evaluate a potential partner, this questionnaire will help you to gauge how well your partner's character traits and behaviours align with the principles outlined in Chapter 7. Your answers will help evaluate various aspects of your relationship or potential partner, guiding you towards informed decisions to support long-term success.

HOW TO COMPLETE THE QUESTIONNAIRE

When answering the questionnaire, please consider the current person you are seeing or reflect on a significant relationship.

If your relationship is very new, start gathering examples to help you gain the clarity needed to complete the questionnaire.

Use the scale below to indicate how well each statement aligns with your observations of a partner's or potential partner's behaviours and views:

1   Not at all
2   Somewhat
3   Moderately
4   Very much
5   Completely

If you have no frame of reference for any of the statements — i.e., you have not gone through the relevant experience with your partner — add a score of 0.

It is important you answer honestly to give you a true picture of the person you are assessing. Make sure you set yourself up in a quiet place and think carefully about your responses, but don't spend too long on each statement, as this can prevent you from providing authentic answers.

SECTION I

These statements are about you. Think about yourself in the relationship.

Category	Statements	Score out of 5
1	I am able to focus on work or personal interests without being overly distracted by thoughts of my partner	
	My happiness does not solely depend on my partner	
	I understand that my partner cannot be perfect in every way	
	I am comfortable spending time alone	
	I am able to maintain my own hobbies, interests and friends outside of the relationship	

SECTION 2

For the next set of statements, think about you and your partner as a couple.

Category	Statements	Score out of 5
2	We are respectful of the way we communicate with one another	
	We understand what success means for both of us	
	We have a good awareness of each other's dreams and aspirations	
	We respect each other's views on religion/spirituality and how this influences our lives	
	We have similar outlooks on work/ life balance and spending time with family	
3	We are aligned on whether we want to be in a long-term relationship	
	We agree on what our ideal future looks like as a couple	
	We are aligned on whether the relationship is monogamous or not	

Category	Statements	Score out of 5
	We are aligned on our views about having and raising children	
	We both openly discuss our finances in order to support our life together	

SECTION 3

For the next set of statements, think about your partner.

Category	Statements	Score out of 5
4	My partner makes a genuine effort to understand my beliefs	
	They are willing to compromise where our opinions differ	
	They are able to open up and share how they feel about the relationship	
	They are respectful of my boundaries and decisions	
	They show a genuine interest in my passions and future plans	

Category	Statements	Score out of 5
5	They demonstrate respect during our intimate moments	
	They frequently check in with me to ensure I'm comfortable during intimate interactions	
	They put effort into maintaining the spark in our sexual relationship	
	They consistently honour the boundaries we've established together	
	They approach discussions about our intimate experiences and histories with understanding and without judgement	
6	They are comfortable opening up about the things that are difficult in their life	
	They provide me with emotional support when I am going through a difficult time	
	They trust me when I am away from them	
	They can admit when they are wrong and say sorry during an argument	
	They do not take their frustrations out on me and instead talk about how they feel	

LONG-TERM RELATIONSHIP SATISFACTION SCALE

Category	Statements	Score out of 5
7	They are able to bounce back from setbacks, challenges and failures quickly	
	They practise daily self-care habits	
	They maintain a positive and realistic perspective during difficult times	
	They encourage me to have a social circle outside of the relationship	
	They focus on solutions, rather than dwelling only on the problem	
8	When things get tough for me, they are able to prioritise me and what I need	
	They create a safe and accepting environment for me to be my true self	
	They treat me with respect and kindness, even during disagreements	
	They do thoughtful things for me without being asked	
	They make time to give me their undivided attention	

Category	Statements	Score out of 5
9	They are willing to step out of their comfort zone when trying new things with me	
	They can hear difficult personal feedback about themselves and act upon it	
	They are a doer, taking action instead of being just a dreamer	
	When I think I can't do something, they encourage me to be brave	
	They bring fresh perspective and insights to our plans for the future	
10	They are open to new experiences, cultures and ideas	
	They enjoy learning and discovering new things about me	
	They take the time to understand a situation before making a snap decision	
	They want to share new experiences with me	
	They refrain from making negative comments about choices or lifestyles that are different from their own	

SCORING

Add up your total score for each category and write them in the spaces below. There are two tables to complete.

RELATIONSHIP DYNAMICS RESULTS TABLE

Category	Add your score here
1. Infatuation	
2. Shared Values	
3. Relationship Goals	
4. Genuine Interest	
5. Aligned Sexual Boundaries	
Total Relationship Dynamics score	

CHARACTER TRAITS RESULTS TABLE

Category	Add your score here
6. Emotional Fitness	
7. Resilient Resourcefulness	
8. Compassionate Support	
9. Courageous Vision	
10. Open-Minded Understanding	
Total Character Traits score	

Add up your scores from the two results tables and enter your total score in the space below, then review your result in the scoring table that follows.

Total Score	

SCORING TABLE

This questionnaire provides an assessment based on your responses, and individual circumstances may vary. It is essential to use these results as a starting point for communication and reflection with your partner, aiming to foster understanding, growth and a healthy relationship.

Tier one shows the strongest result and tier three the weakest:

LONG-TERM RELATIONSHIP SATISFACTION SCALE

Tier	Scoring	Description
1	190 or above	Your score indicates a high likelihood of a fulfilling long-term relationship. You and your partner demonstrate strong compatibility, positive dynamics, and the essential qualities needed for a lasting bond.
2	151 – 189	Your score indicates an average likelihood of a fulfilling long-term relationship. There are areas that could benefit from further attention and growth, but with effort and communication you have the potential to strengthen your connection.
3	150 or below	Your score suggests a lower likelihood of a long-term relationship. It may be important to address the areas that need improvement and consider whether your compatibility aligns with your long-term goals.

BREAKDOWN OF CATEGORIES

For all categories, a high score refers to a score of 19 and above, and a low score to 15 and below.

RELATIONSHIP DYNAMICS

Category 1	Infatuation	Infatuation can influence your perception of a relationship. Low scores can indicate you look at the relationship with rose-tinted glasses. If this is the case, take some time to consider what your relationship is actually like and think about the behaviours that are being displayed.
Category 2	Shared Values	A high score indicates a strong alignment and understanding of fundamental beliefs, guiding principles and goals. If you as a couple have a high score in this category, you are likely to experience deeper emotional connections, enhanced communication and long-lasting harmony in your relationship.

| Category 3 | Relationship Goals | A high score demonstrates a profound alignment on crucial aspects of your partnership. You share a mutual desire for commitment, openly discuss building a life together, and have a unified vision on monogamy and parenthood. Additionally, you value shared financial planning and responsibilities. This strong foundation of shared values fosters trust, unity and commitment, contributing to a lasting and fulfilling relationship. |
| Category 4 | Genuine Interest | High scores indicate your significant other is interested in getting to know the real you. They respect your boundaries and are able to clearly communicate with you. |

Category 5	Aligned Sexual Boundaries	High scores in this area highlight a relationship built on mutual respect, understanding and communication within intimate moments. Such a relationship prioritises comfort, respect and established boundaries, and facilitates open discussions about intimacy without judgement.

CHARACTER TRAITS

Category 6	Emotional Fitness	A high score indicates a partner who feels comfortable sharing their feelings with you in an open and honest way, expresses their true emotions, provides emotional support when needed, engages in emotional conversations, validates your emotions, and resolves conflicts in a healthy and respectful manner.

Category 7	Resilient Resourcefulness	A high score indicates your significant other navigates and overcomes challenges resiliently, provides support and encouragement during difficult times, communicates their frustrations without taking it out on you, reaches out for help when facing difficulties, practises self-care and maintains well-being habits, demonstrates a willingness to learn and grow from challenges, and avoids holding on to negativity.
Category 8	Compassionate Support	A high score indicates your significant other prioritises your needs, especially in tough times. They foster an environment where you can genuinely be yourself, ensuring that respect and kindness underscore all interactions. They often surprise you with their thoughtfulness and ensure dedicated time for you. Moreover, they maintain a positive atmosphere, even in challenging circumstances.

Category 9	Courageous Vision	A high score indicates your significant other embraces challenges, readily stepping beyond their comfort zones, especially with you. They value feedback and are proactive in acting on it, choosing action over mere contemplation. When doubt creeps in, they're your pillar of encouragement, and they stand by their decisions and commitments. Furthermore, they constantly infuse fresh perspectives, enriching your shared visions for the future.
Category 10	Open-Minded Under-standing	A high score indicates your partner is open-minded, curious about diverse cultures and ideas, and keen to learn more about you. They're self-aware, they enjoy sharing new experiences and they ask meaningful questions. Most importantly, they avoid making snap judgements and respect differing lifestyles and choices.

RESOURCES

BOOKS

Adult Attachment: Theory, Research, and Clinical Implications by W. Steven Rholes and Jeffry A. Simpson (Guilford Press, 2004)

The All-or-Nothing Marriage: How the Best Marriages Work by Eli J. Finkel (E.P. Dutton, 2017)

The Art of Seduction by Robert Greene (Profile, 2001)

Attached: Are You Anxious, Avoidant or Secure? How the Science of Adult Attachment Can Help You Find – and Keep – Love by Amir Levine and Rachel S.F. Heller (Bluebird, 2019)

Bad Men: The Hidden Roots of Sexual Deception, Harassment and Assault by David M. Buss (Robinson, 2021)

The Body Keeps the Score: Brain, Mind, and Body in the Healing of Trauma by Bessel van der Kolk (Viking, 2014)

Eight Dates: Essential Conversations for a Lifetime of Love by John Gottman et al. (Workman, 2019)

Finding Love Again: 6 Simple Steps to a New and Happy Relationship by Terri L. Orbuch (Sourcebooks Casablanca, 2012)

The Five Love Languages: How to Express Heartfelt Commitment to Your Mate by Gary Chapman (Northfield Publishing, 1992)

5 Simple Steps to Take Your Marriage from Good to Great by Terri L. Orbuch (River Grove Books, 2015)

Friends: Understanding the Power of Our Most Important Relationships by Robin Dunbar (Little, Brown, 2021)

Generations: The Real Differences Between Gen Z, Millennials, Gen X, Boomers, and Silents – and What They Mean for America's Future by Jean M. Twenge (Atria Books, 2023)

The Good Life: Lessons from the World's Longest Study on Happiness by Robert Waldinger and Marc Schulz (Rider, 2023)

Hold Me Tight: Seven Conversations for a Lifetime of Love by Sue Johnson (Little, Brown, 2008)

Influence: The Psychology of Persuasion by Robert B. Cialdini (Harper Business, 2021)

Love Factually: 10 Proven Steps from I Wish to I Do by Duana C. Welch (LoveScience Media, 2022)

Mating in Captivity: Unlocking Erotic Intelligence by Esther Perel (Hodder & Stoughton, 2007)

Mindset: Changing the Way You Think to Fulfil Your Potential by Carol S. Dweck (Robinson, 2017)

Of Boys and Men: Why the Modern Male Is Struggling, Why It Matters, and What to Do About It by Richard V. Reeves (Swift Press, 2022)

The Paradox of Choice: Why More Is Less by Barry Schwartz (HarperCollins, 2004)

Predictably Irrational: The Hidden Forces That Shape Our Decisions by Dan Ariely (HarperCollins, 2008)

The Seven Principles for Making Marriage Work by John M. Gottman and Nan Silver (Orion Spring, 2018)

The Weirdest People in the World: How the West Became Psychologically Peculiar and Particularly Prosperous by Joseph Henrich (Allen Lane, 2020)

When the Body Says No: Understanding the Stress-Disease Connection by Gabor Maté (John Wiley & Sons, 2003)

DOMESTIC ABUSE ORGANISATIONS

In the UK, you can find a number of organisations via the **NHS website**: https://www.nhs.uk/live-well/getting-help-for-domestic-violence/

In addition, **Women's Aid** is a leading domestic abuse charity in the UK. They offer a range of services to support women and children experiencing domestic violence, including a twenty-four-hour helpline, safety planning assistance and refuge accommodation. You can contact the National Domestic Abuse Helpline on 0808 2000 247 or visit the Women's Aid website at www.womensaid. org.uk.

The **National Domestic Violence Hotline** in the United States provides 24/7 confidential support, information and resources for individuals experiencing domestic violence. They can help you develop a safety plan, provide crisis intervention and connect you with local services. You can reach them by calling 1-800-799-SAFE (7233) or visiting their website at www.thehotline.org.

The **National Network to End Domestic Violence** is a US-based organisation that focuses on providing resources, support and advocacy for domestic violence victims. Their website offers information on safety planning, legal resources and access to local domestic violence organisations. Visit their website at www.nnedv.org for more information.

NOTES

CHAPTER I: FROM ARRANGED MARRIAGES TO ATTACHMENT THEORY AND BEYOND

1 Maslow, A.H., 'A theory of human motivation', *Psychological Review* 50(4) (1943): 370–96.

2 Finkel, E.J., *The All-or-Nothing Marriage: How the Best Marriages Work* (E.P. Dutton, 2017).

3 Schwartz, B., *The Paradox of Choice: Why More Is Less* (HarperCollins, 2004).

4 See Finkel, *The All-or-Nothing Marriage*; Coontz, S., *Marriage, a History: How Love Conquered Marriage* (Penguin, 2006); and Buss, D.M., *Evolutionary Psychology: The New Science of the Mind* (Routledge, 2019).

5 Finkel, *The All-or-Nothing Marriage*.

6 Rosenfeld, M.J., 'Who wants the breakup? Gender and breakup in heterosexual couples' in Alwin, D.F., Felmlee, D. and Kreager, D. (eds), *Social Networks and the Life Course: Integrating the Development of Human Lives and Social Relational Networks* (Springer, 2018): 221–43.

7 Finkel, *The All-or-Nothing Marriage*.

8 Waldinger, R. and Schulz, M., *The Good Life: Lessons from the World's Longest Study on Happiness* (Rider, 2023).

9 Rholes, W.S. and Simpson, J.A., *Adult Attachment: Theory, Research, and Clinical Implications* (Guilford Press, 2004).

10 Firestone, L., 'How your attachment style impacts your relationship', PsychAlive: https://www.psychalive.org/how-your-attachment-style-impacts-your-relationship/.

11 Van Buren, A. and Cooley, E.L., 'Attachment styles, view of self and negative affect', *North American Journal of Psychology*, 4(3) (2002): 417–30.

12 Levine, A. and Heller, R.S.F., *Attached: Are You Anxious, Avoidant or Secure? How the Science of Adult Attachment Can Help You Find – and Keep – Love* (Bluebird, 2019).

13 Jaiswal, T., *Indian Arranged Marriages: A Social Psychological Perspective* (Routledge, 2014).

14 Ariely, D., *Predictably Irrational: The Hidden Forces That Shape Our Decisions* (HarperCollins, 2008).

15 Dunbar, R., *Friends: Understanding the Power of Our Most Important Relationships* (Little, Brown, 2021).

16 Ibid.

CHAPTER 2: THE POWER OF OUR PASTS AND THE HIDDEN FACTORS THAT SHAPE OUR RELATIONSHIPS

1 Maté, G., *When the Body Says No: Understanding the Stress-Disease Connection* (John Wiley & Sons, 2003).

2 Maté, G. and Maté, D., *The Myth of Normal: Trauma, Illness, and Healing in a Toxic Culture* (Vermilion, 2022).

3 Van der Kolk, B., *The Body Keeps the Score: Brain, Mind, and Body in the Healing of Trauma* (Viking, 2014).

4 Dweck, C.S., *Mindset: Changing the Way You Think to Fulfil Your Potential* (Robinson, 2017).

5 Jackson, C., 'Does counselling make a difference?' *Therapy Today* 27(6) (2016): https://www.bacp.co.uk/bacp-journals/therapy-today/2016/july-2016/does-counselling-make-a-difference/.

6 Maté, *The Myth of Normal*.

7 Tinder, *The Future of Dating 2023*: https://filecache.mediaroom.com/mr5mr_tinder/179342/Copy_of_FOD_Report_2023_FINAL.pdf.

8 Dunbar, R., *Friends: Understanding the Power of Our Most Important Relationships* (Little, Brown, 2021).

CHAPTER 3: A STRONG SENSE OF SELF IS THE KEY TO A SUCCESSFUL RELATIONSHIP

1 Seligman, M.E.P. and Csikszentmihalyi, M., 'Positive psychology: An introduction', *American Psychologist* 55(1) (2000): 5 – 14.

2 Kinderman, P., Schwannauer, M., Pontin, E. and Tai, S., 'The development and validation of a general measure of well-being: The BBC well-being scale', *Quality of Life Research* 20(7) (2011): 1035 – 1042.

3 Sustainable Development Solutions Network, *World Happiness Report 2023*: https://worldhappiness.report/.

4 Ryff, C.D. and Singer, B., 'Know thyself and become what you are: A eudaimonic approach to psychological well-being', *Journal of Happiness Studies* 9(1) (2008): 13 – 39.

5 Finkel, E.J. et al., 'The suffocation model: Why marriage in America is becoming an all-or-nothing institution', *Current Directions in Psychological Science* 24(3) (2015): 238 – 44.

6 Waldinger, R. and Schulz, M., *The Good Life: Lessons from the World's Longest Study on Happiness* (Rider, 2023).

7 Fletcher, G., Simpson, J.A., Campbell, L. and Overall, N.C., *The Science of Intimate Relationships*, 2nd edn (Wiley-Blackwell, 2019).

8 Finkel, E.J., *The All-or-Nothing Marriage: How the Best Marriages Work* (E.P. Dutton, 2017).

9 Kounang, N., 'What is the science behind fear?' CNN Health (29 October 2015): https://edition.cnn.com/2015/10/29/health/science-of-fear/.

10 Bardi, A. and Schwartz, S.H., 'Values and behavior: Strength and structure of relations', *Personality and Social Psychology Bulletin* 29(10) (2003): 1207 – 1220.

11 Caughlin, J.P. and Huston, T.L., 'Communication in families and romantic relationships: Recent research developments and future prospects', *Journal of Family Communication* 6(2) (2006): 159 – 69.

12 Twenge, J.M., *Generations: The Real Differences Between Gen Z, Millennials, Gen X, Boomers, and Silents – and What They Mean for America's Future* (Atria Books, 2023).

CHAPTER 4: HOW YOUR ENVIRONMENT SHAPES YOUR SEARCH FOR A PARTNER

1 Confer, J.C. et al., 'Evolutionary psychology. Controversies, questions, prospects, and limitations', *American Psychologist* 65(2) (2010): 110−26.

2 Lippa, R.A., 'The preferred traits of mates in a cross-national study of heterosexual and homosexual men and women: An examination of biological and cultural influences', *Archives of Sexual Behavior* 36(2) (2007): 193−208.

3 Buss, D.M. and Schmitt, D.P., 'Sexual strategies theory: An evolutionary perspective on human mating', *Psychological Review* 100(2) (1993): 204−32.

4 Henrich, J., *The Weirdest People in the World: How the West Became Psychologically Peculiar and Particularly Prosperous* (Allen Lane, 2020).

5 Farrelly, D., Owens, R., Elliott, H.R., Walden, H. and Wetherell, M., 'The effects of being in a "new relationship" on levels of testosterone in men', *Evolutionary Psychology* 13(1) (2015): 250−61.

6 Gettler, L.T., McDade, T.W., Feranil, A.B. and Kuzawa, C.W., 'Longitudinal evidence that fatherhood decreases testosterone in human males', *Proceedings of the National Academy of Sciences* 108(39) (2011): 16194−9.

7 Singh, D., 'Adaptive significance of female physical attractiveness: Role of waist-to-hip ratio', *Journal of Personality and Social Psychology* 65(2) (1993): 293−307.

8 Eastwick, P.W., Luchies, L.B., Finkel, E.J. and Hunt, L.L., 'The many voices of Darwin's descendants: Reply to Puts and Bailey', *Psychological Science* 25(9) (2014): 1790−92.

9 Forgas, J.P. and Laham, S.M., 'Halo Effects' in Pohl, R.F. (ed.), *Cognitive Illusions: Intriguing Phenomena in Judgement, Thinking and Memory* (Psychology Press, 2016).

10 Thompson, D., 'Colleges have a guy problem', *Atlantic* (14 September 2021).

11 Poston, D.L. and Glover, K.S., 'Too many males: Marriage market implications of gender imbalances in China', *Genus* 61(2) (2005): 119−40.

12 Garvey, M., 'Knowledge of yourself' (interview *c.*1924): https://www.facebook.com/watch/?v=362552327748268.

13 Regents of the University of Michigan, *Monitoring the Future*: Retrieved from https://monitoringthefuture.org/.

14 ElHage, A., 'Do today's teens see marriage and children in their future?', Institute for Family Studies (12 October 2022): https://ifstudies.org/blog/do-todays-teens-see-marriage-and-children-in-their-future.

15 Gendler, A., 'The history of marriage', TED-Ed (13 February 2014): https://www.youtube.com/watch?v=ZZZ6QB5TSfk.

CHAPTER 5: THE PROS AND CONS OF DIFFERENT WAYS TO MEET A PARTNER

1 Finkel, E.J., *The All-or-Nothing Marriage: How the Best Marriages Work* (E.P. Dutton, 2017).

2 Johnson, S., *Hold Me Tight: Seven Conversations for a Lifetime of Love* (Little, Brown, 2008).

3 Perel, E., *Mating in Captivity: Unlocking Erotic Intelligence* (Hodder & Stoughton, 2007).

4 Vogels, E.A. and Mcclain, C., 'Key findings about online dating in the U.S.', Pew Research Center (2 February 2023): https://www.pewresearch.org/short-reads/2023/02/02/key-findings-about-online-dating-in-the-u-s/.

5 Lichter, D.T., LeClere, F.B. and McLaughlin, D.K., 'Local marriage markets and the marital behavior of black and white women', *American Journal of Sociology* 96(4) (1991): 843 – 67.

6 Hitsch, G.J., Hortaçsu, A. and Ariely, D., 'What makes you click? Mate preferences and matching outcomes in online dating', *MIT Sloan Research Paper No. 4603–06* (2006).

7 Finkel, E.J., Eastwick, P.W., Karney, B.R., Reis, H.T. and Sprecher, S., 'Online dating: A critical analysis from the perspective of psychological science', *Psychological Science in the Public Interest* 13(1) (2012): 3 – 66.

8 Granovetter, M.S., 'The strength of weak ties', *American Journal of Sociology* 78(6) (1973): 1360 – 80.

9 Dunbar, R.I.M., 'Neocortex size as a constraint on group size in primates', *Journal of Human Evolution* 22(6) (1992): 469 – 93.

10 Gillies, Trent, 'How to surf the Web for a mate: eHarmony founder', CNBC (9 May 2015): https://www.cnbc.com/2015/05/08/how-to-surf-the-web-for-a-mate-eharmony-founder.html

11 Dixon, S.J., 'Most popular dating apps worldwide in July 2023, by number of monthly downloads', Statista (8 August 2023): https://www.statista.com/statistics/1200234/most-popular-dating-apps-worldwide-by-number-of-downloads/.

12 Tinder, *The Future of Dating 2023*: https://filecache.mediaroom.com/mr5mr_tinder/179342/Copy_of_FOD_Report_2023_FINAL.pdf.

13 Karimi, F. and Souza, S., 'Instagram influencer scammed over $2 million from older, lonely Americans, federal prosecutors say', CNN (16 May 2023): https://edition.cnn.com/2023/05/16/us/mona-montrage-alleged-romance-scammer-cec/.

14 Tinder, *The Future of Dating 2023*.

15 Avery, J. and Greenwald, R., 'A new approach to building your personal brand', *Harvard Business Review* (May–June 2023): https://hbr.org/2023/05/a-new-approach-to-building-your-personal-brand.

CHAPTER 6: MAXIMISING YOUR CHANCES OF FINDING A PARTNER

1 Fowers, B.J. and Owenz, M.B., 'A eudaimonic theory of marital quality', *Journal of Family Theory & Review* 2(4) (2010): 334–52.

2 Apostolou, M., Argyridou, M., Nikoloudi, E.E. and Lajunen, T.J., 'I want our relationship to last: Strategies that people employ in order to improve their intimate relationships', *Evolutionary Psychology* 20(4) (2010): 14747049221147154.

3 Kashdan, T.B. and Roberts, J.E., 'Trait and state curiosity in the genesis of intimacy: Differentiation from related constructs', *Journal of Social and Clinical Psychology* 23(6) (2004): 792–816.

4 Tinder, *The Future of Dating 2023*: https://filecache.mediaroom.com/mr5mr_tinder/179342/Copy_of_FOD_Report_2023_FINAL.pdf

5 YouGov, 'How Brits meet their partners', (2023): https://yougov.co.uk/topics/relationships/trackers/how-brits-meet-their-partners.

6 Cialdini, R.B., *Influence: The Psychology of Persuasion* (Harper Business, 2021).

7 Ibid.

8 Reeves, R.V., *Of Boys and Men: Why the Modern Male Is Struggling, Why It Matters, and What to Do About It* (Swift Press, 2022).

CHAPTER 7: GREEN FLAGS: THE FIVE FUNDAMENTALS YOU SHOULD BE LOOKING FOR IN A PARTNER

1 Hatcher, K., 'Kim Kardashian shares a list of what she's looking for in a man: "No heavy baggage, I have enough"', *People* (25 May 2023):https://people.com/kim-kardashian-list-what-she-is-looking-for-in-a-man-7503986.

2 Stewart, S., Stinnett, H. and Rosenfeld, L.B., 'Sex differences in desired characteristics of short-term and long-term relationship partners', *Journal of Social and Personal Relationships* 17(6) (2000): 843−53.

3 Trivers, R., 'Parental investment and sexual selection', in Campbell, B.G. (ed.), *Sexual Selection and the Descent of Man* (Routledge, 1972).

4 Shtatfeld, R. and Barak, A., 'Factors related to initiating interpersonal contacts on internet dating sites: A view from the social exchange theory', *Interpersona* 3(2) (2009): 19−37.

5 Fein, E. and Schneider, S., *The Rules: Time-Tested Secrets for Capturing the Heart of Mr. Right* (Grand Central Publishing, 1995).

6 Chapman, G., *The Five Love Languages: How to Express Heartfelt Commitment to Your Mate* (Northfield Publishing, 1992).

7 Aron, A. et al., 'The self-expansion model of motivation and cognition in close relationships' in Simpson, J. A. and Campbell, L. (eds), *The Oxford Handbook of Close Relationships* (Oxford University Press, 2013).

8 Meyer, D. and Sledge, R., 'The relationship between conflict topics and romantic relationship dynamics', *Journal of Family Issues* 43(2) (2022): 306−323.

9 Miczo, N. and Averbeck, J.M., 'Perceived partner humor use and relationship satisfaction in romantic pairs: The mediating role of relational uncertainty', *HUMOR* 33(4) (2020): 513−34.

10 Niehuis, S., Skogrand, L. and Huston, T.L., 'When marriages die: Premarital and early marital precursors to divorce', *Forum for Family and Consumer Issues*, 11(1) (2006): 1–7.

11 Willis, J. and Todorov, A., 'First impressions: Making up your mind after a 100-Ms exposure to a face', *Psychological Science* 17(7) (2006): 592–8.

CHAPTER 8: RED FLAGS: HOW TO IDENTIFY TOXIC PARTNERS

1 Buss, D.M., *Bad Men: The Hidden Roots of Sexual Deception, Harassment and Assault* (Robinson, 2021).

2 Paulhus, D.L. and Williams, K.M., 'The dark triad of personality: Narcissism, Machiavellianism, and psychopathy', *Journal of Research in Personality* 36(6) (2002): 556–63.

3 American Psychiatric Association, *Diagnostic and Statistical Manual of Mental Disorders, Fifth Edition, Text Revision* (American Psychiatric Association Publishing, 2022).

4 Ackerman, R.A., Donnellan, M.B. and Wright, A.G.C., 'Current conceptualizations of narcissism', *Current Opinion in Psychiatry* 32(1) (2019): 32–7.

5 Jonason, P.K., Li, N.P., Webster, G.D. and Schmitt, D.P., 'The dark triad: Facilitating a short-term mating strategy in men', *European Journal of Personality* 23(1) (2009): 5–18.

6 Machiavelli, N., *The Prince* (Oxford University Press, 2008).

7 Greene, R., *The Art of Seduction* (Profile, 2001).

8 Strauss, N., *The Game: Undercover in the Secret Society of Pickup Artists* (Canongate, 2005).

9 Mitra, P. and Fluyau, D., *Narcissistic Personality Disorder* (StatPearls Publishing, 2023).

10 Monaghan, C., Bizumic, B., Williams, T. and Sellbom, M., 'Two-dimensional Machiavellianism: Conceptualization, theory, and measurement of the views and tactics dimensions', *Psychological Assessment* 32(3) (2020): 277–93.

11 Blair, J., Mitchell, D. and Blair, K., *The Psychopath: Emotion and the Brain* (Blackwell, 2005).

12 Braithwaite J. et al., 'The basis of clinical tribalism, hierarchy and stereotyping: a laboratory-controlled teamwork experiment', *BMJ Open* 6(7) (2016): e012467.

13 Buss, *Bad Men*.

CHAPTER 9: ARE YOU READY FOR FOREVER? UNDERSTANDING THE SIGNS OF COMMITMENT READINESS

1 Carrère, S., Buehlman, K.T., Gottman, J.M., Coan, J.A. and Ruck-stuhl, L., 'Predicting marital stability and divorce in newlywed couples', *Journal of Family Psychology* 14(1) (2000): 42 – 58.

2 Hatfield, E., Utne, M.K. and Traupmann, J., 'Equity theory and intimate relationships', in Burgess, R.L. and Huston, T.L. (eds), *Social Exchange in Developing Relationships* (Academic Press, 1979).

3 Lin, I.-F., Brown, S.L. and Hammersmith, A.M., 'Marital biography, social security, and poverty', Research on Aging 39(1) (2017): 86 – 110.

ABOUT THE AUTHOR

© Christopher Bethell

Paul Carrick Brunson is a renowned relationship counsellor, matchmaker, television host and author who
specialises in the science of interpersonal relationships
and personal development. His expertise has earned him
international recognition, and he currently serves as the
co-host of *Married at First Sight UK* and *Celebs Go Dating*, in
addition to being the relationship expert for *Lorraine* and
Good Morning America.

As the Global Relationship Insights Expert for Tinder, the world's largest dating app, Paul is at the forefront of the digital dating revolution. Oprah Winfrey has also praised his work and selected him as a host of the show *Lovetown, USA*, which examined the transformative power of love, grace, kindness and forgiveness on an entire community.

Paul is a serial entrepreneur and former business columnist for *USA TODAY*, where he shared his insights on entrepreneurship and relationship building. He was also the host of the *Better with Paul* podcasts, where he revealed his vast knowledge and experience in navigating life and business.

In addition to his work in the media, Paul is passionate about impacting lives through the application of relationship science. He is dedicated to mentoring a new generation of servant-leaders with a desire to change the world. He is the founder and chair of Give Love Build Hope, a non-profit organisation dedicated to transforming schools in rural areas of the Caribbean.

Paul is a proud second-generation son of Jamaica, and he takes great pride in his roles as a husband and father. When he's not busy changing the world, Paul can often be found with a good book in one hand and a Red Stripe beer in the other.